D0264198

# THANK YOU FOR THIS MOMENT

# VALÉRIE TRIERWEILER

*A story of love, power and betrayal*

TRANSLATED BY
CLÉMENCE SEBAG

WITHDRAWN
FROM STOCK

**Biteback Publishing**

This edition published in Great Britain in 2015 by
Biteback Publishing Ltd
Westminster Tower
3 Albert Embankment
London SE1 7SP
Copyright © Valérie Trierweiler 2014, 2015

Copyright in the translation © Clémence Sebag 2014, 2015

Originally published in France in 2014 by Les Arènes

Valérie Trierweiler has asserted her right under the Copyright, Designs and
Patents Act 1988 to be identified as the author of this work.

All rights reserved. No part of this publication may be reproduced, stored
in a retrieval system or transmitted, in any form or by any means, without
the publisher's prior permission in writing.

This book is sold subject to the condition that it shall not, by way of trade
or otherwise, be lent, resold, hired out or otherwise circulated without the
publisher's prior consent in any form of binding or cover other than that
in which it is published and without a similar condition, including this
condition, being imposed on the subsequent purchaser.

Every reasonable effort has been made to trace copyright holders of
material reproduced in this book, but if any have been inadvertently
overlooked the publishers would be glad to hear from them.

ISBN 978-1-84954-864-9

10 9 8 7 6 5 4 3 2 1

A CIP catalogue record for this book is available from the British Library.

Set in Adobe Garamond Pro

Printed and bound in Great Britain by
CPI Group (UK) Ltd, Croydon CR0 4YY

Laois County Library
Leabharlann Chontae Laoise

MIX
Paper from
responsible sources
FSC
www.fsc.org
FSC® C020471

Acc. No. ...15/ 3423....

Class No. ...920 Tri.........

Inv. No. ...13118...........

*To you three,*

*To my three,*

*To all three.*

# PUBLISHER'S FOREWORD

THIS IS NO ordinary memoir. It tells the story of a love affair that went very wrong. The author bares her soul in a way that is at times painful and searing. It is a story that needs to be read by anyone wishing to understand the personality, character and motivations of the man who rules France, François Hollande. But it is no ordinary story Valérie Trierweiler tells. She cannot easily be dismissed as a woman scorned. Yes, she hurts. That much is clear. But in fifteen years of publishing, I have never come across such an honest account of a relationship which was so key to a politician coming to power and then seemingly not having a clue what to do with power once he had achieved it. It is a story of passion and rejection, of power-plays and grandstanding. When I first read it, I read it in one sitting. I found the story and emotion compelling and that is why I wanted to bring it to English-language readers.

This is the first book I have published which doesn't contain any chapters. The original French volume had no chapters, so I felt it should be the same '*en Anglais*'. When Valérie explained to me why she had written it in this way, I understood. It is her story and she felt that it should be one continuous text with no artificial interruption. Who am I to disagree?

I want to thank Valérie for having had the courage to put pen to paper when many advised her to remain silent, for her fortitude in the face of onslaughts from a vicious French media, and, above all, for being herself. When I travelled to Paris to meet her, a few weeks before this book was published, I didn't know what to expect. Would the woman whose words I had read bear any relation to the woman I was about to meet? We met over what turned out to be the best meal I have ever eaten, at a restaurant called Itinéraires in the Latin Quarter, not far from Notre Dame. Despite my lack of French and her lack of English, I hope she realised that Biteback and I are her perfect publishing partners in the UK. I'm very grateful to her for entrusting us with the publication of *Thank You for This Moment*.

I would also like to thank Clémence Sebag for her excellent work in translating the book having been given a very challenging timetable. She has done an excellent job, and has captured Valérie's 'voice' in such a brilliant way.

Finally, let me pay tribute to a lady called Anna Jarota. She is Valérie's literary agent and brought her book to Biteback. Let's just say she has restored my faith in literary agents and has been an absolute pleasure to deal with. I look forward to a continuing working relationship.

Now, over to Valérie...

*Iain Dale*
*London, November 2014*

# FOREWORD

'YOU MUST LAY yourself bare before the public gaze.' A piece of advice from Philippe Labro when François Hollande was elected. Philippe is someone I have a lot of respect for – a writer, a media man – but I never found a way to be an open book, as he recommended. I could not bring myself to show who I really was. Unveiling aspects of my life, talking about my family and my relationship with the President was out of the question. I did the opposite, in fact – I locked everything up and drew the bolt.

Which didn't prevent journalists from writing and talking – about a woman who bore very little resemblance to me. More often than not, they simply did not know the facts; at other times they were angling for a scandal. A couple of dozen books, even more magazine covers, and thousands of articles were printed – distorting carnival mirrors that reflected second-guesses and hearsay, when they weren't pure fantasy. The woman in the mirror had my name and my face but she was unrecognisable to me. It felt like it was not just my personal life that was being stolen but my sense of identity.

Protected by my armour, I believed I could withstand anything and everything. As attacks became increasingly violent, I shut down further. The French saw my frozen, sometimes tense face. They did not understand. It came to the point where I could no longer bear to go out in the street – I could not handle the way passers-by looked at me.

Then – in just a few hours in January 2014 – my life was devastated and my future shattered into a million tiny pieces. Suddenly, I was alone, stunned and grief-stricken. It became obvious to me that the only way of regaining control over the narrative of my life was to narrate it. I was misunderstood – sullied, even – and I suffered from it.

I decided to smash through the dam I had built – I decided to put pen to paper and tell my story, the real story. Where I had once fought tirelessly to protect my privacy, I now had to relinquish that in part – to hand over the keys to unlock me and make sense of it all. Every piece in this absurd puzzle fits. I was thirsty for the truth – I needed it to overcome this hurdle and move on. I owed it to my children, to my family, to those close to me. Writing had become a vital need. Night and day for months, I silently 'laid myself bare'…

'The silence of your loved one is a quiet crime'

Tahar Ben Jelloun

THE FIRST MESSAGE came in on Wednesday morning. A friend of mine who is a journalist sent me notice: 'It looks like *Closer* is going to publish a picture of François and Gayet on Friday.' My reply was brief – it hardly mattered to me. The rumour had been poisoning my life for months. It came and went, and came back again, and I simply could not bring myself to believe it. I forwarded the message to François, without further comment. He replied immediately: 'Who told you that?'

'That's not the issue,' I said, 'the issue is whether you have done something wrong or not.'

'No, I haven't.'

I was reassured.

And yet, as the day progressed the rumour persisted. François and I spoke in the afternoon and had dinner together without broaching the subject. The rumour had already caused arguments between us – no need to make things worse. The next morning I received a text message along the same lines from another journalist friend.

'Hi Val. The Gayet rumour is rearing its head again. It looks like it is going to make the cover of *Closer* tomorrow – but I imagine you know that already.'

Again I forwarded the message to François. This time there was no reply. He was away – just outside of Paris, in Creil – on business with the army.

I asked one of my old journalist friends who still had some contacts within the tabloid press to keep an eye out for any news. Calls kept coming in to the Élysée from editorial staff. All of the President's PR advisers were being harassed with questions by journalists about this hypothetical magazine cover.

The morning was spent talking to my nearest and dearest. I was scheduled to join the team of the Élysée nursery for a meal prepared by the children's cook. We had started this ritual the year before. A dozen women took care of both the Élysée staff's children and the children of the President's advisers. A month earlier we had celebrated

Christmas together with the parents of the children in the nursery. François and I handed out the presents – he had left in a hurry, as usual, while I stayed talking to everyone. It was like a harbour of peace I felt content in.

I was excited about the lunch but I felt stifled – as if I sensed that a danger was fast approaching. The nursery head was waiting for us by the door, across the street from the Élysée. Patrice Biancone, a former Radio France Internationale colleague who had become my loyal Chief of Staff, came with me. When I arrived I took my two mobile phones out of my pocket – one for work and the public sphere, the other for François, my children, my family and my close friends. The table was laid out for a party, the faces around me shone with happiness. I hid my unease and put my personal mobile next to my plate. Fred the cook brought us his dishes, while the childminders bustled around the tables, taking turns watching the little ones.

In 2015 the Élysée nursery will celebrate its thirtieth birthday. Nearly 600 children have been in that nursery, including the President's children, back when he was an adviser at the Élysée. To celebrate this event, I had planned to reunite the former babies – grown men and women now. After twenty years working for *Paris-Match* I had no trouble visualising the pretty picture such a gathering at the Élysée would make.

We wanted to rename the nursery after Danielle

Mitterrand, who had set it up in October 1985. Now that I was an ambassador of the *France Libertés* foundation, I was in charge of organising the anniversary. I promised I would soon send out a note to François Hollande's Chief of Staff Sylvie Hubac so she could endorse the project and give us a budget.

My phone started to vibrate. My journalist friend had been 'fishing for information' and was messaging to confirm that *Closer* planned a cover picture of François just outside Julie Gayet's flat. My heart exploded. I tried not to betray what was going through my mind. I handed my phone to Patrice Biancone so he could read the message. I did not keep secrets from him: 'Look, it's about that topic we were discussing earlier.' I kept the tone of my voice as flat as possible. We had been friends for twenty years and a simple glance was enough for us to understand one another. I tried to sound detached: 'We'll deal with it later.'

I tried to focus on talking to the nursery staff, while thoughts tumbled through my brain. They had been hit by a chickenpox epidemic. Nodding enthusiastically, I sent François a text about the *Closer* info. It was no longer a rumour, it was now a fact.

He replied almost instantly: 'Meet me at the flat at 3 p.m.'

The time came to say goodbye to the nursery school head. I had only one street to cross – such a tiny little street – but it seemed like the most dangerous road I have ever walked across. It felt like I was crossing a motorway with my eyes closed, even though only authorised vehicles were admitted.

I walked up the stairs leading to the private apartment at a brisk pace. François was already in our room – our room with its high windows looking onto the centenary trees in the park. We sat on the bed. Each of us on the side we were used to sleeping on. I was only able to utter a single word: 'So?'

'So it's true,' he said.

'What's true? You're sleeping with that girl?'

'Yes,' he admitted, half reclining to lean on his forearm.

We were sat quite close to one another on the spacious bed. I could not get him to look me in the eye, he persistently avoided my gaze. I hurled questions at him: 'How did it happen? Why? When did it start?'

'A month ago,' he claimed.

I remained calm; I did not get angry or shout. And there was certainly no broken china as rumour has it – I am allegedly responsible for millions of euros of imaginary damage.

I could not begin to imagine the tidal wave that was building up.

Could he say that he had only had dinner at her flat, I wondered?

It would never fly. He knew that the picture had been taken after a night he had spent in the rue du Cirque.

What about a Clintonesque scenario? Public apologies, a promise never to see her again. We could start over. I was not prepared to lose him.

His lies started to surface, the truth gradually emerged. He confessed that the affair had been going on for longer. From one month, we reached three, then six, nine, and finally a year.

'We are not strong enough, you will never be able to forgive me,' he said.

Then he went back to his desk for a meeting. I could not face keeping my appointment and asked Patrice Bian-cone to see my visitor for me. I stayed locked up in the room all afternoon. I tried to imagine what would happen, my eyes glued to my phone, checking Twitter updates for glimpses of the scoop that had been announced. I tried to find out more about the tone of the 'photo-reportage'. I texted my closest friends and let my children and my mother know what was going to come out. I did not want them to hear about the scandal in the press. They had to be prepared for it.

François was back for dinner. We met in our room. He seemed more down than I was. I found him kneeling on the bed. He put his head in his hands. He was in a state of shock: 'What are we going to do?'

He surreptitiously used the word 'we' in a story I no longer really belonged in. It was the last time – soon it would be all 'me, me, me'. After our talk, we tried to have dinner in the living room, on the coffee table, as we normally did when we wanted some privacy or when we wanted to have a shorter meal.

I couldn't eat a thing. I tried to find out more. I listed the political consequences. Where was the 'model President'? A President cannot lead two wars if he runs off at every opportunity to see an actress down the road. A President does not behave this way when factories are shutting down, unemployment is rising and his popularity ratings are at their lowest ever. In that moment, I felt more concerned by the potential political damage than by our personal shipwreck. No doubt I still hoped to save our relationship. François asked me to stop my inventory of the disastrous consequences – he knew it all. He gulped down a few mouthfuls and returned to his desk.

He left me alone with my torment; meanwhile he had called a meeting I knew nothing about. 'They' prepared to discuss my fate, without bothering to keep me informed of the ins and outs. François came home at half past ten. He refused to answer my questions. He seemed lost, disorientated. I phoned the Secretary General of the Élysée Pierre-René Lemas and told him I wanted to see him. François asked me what I wanted with him.

'I don't know. I need to see someone.'

It was my turn to use the quasi-secret corridor that leads from the private apartment to the presidential floor. As soon as I arrived, Pierre-René wrapped me in his arms. I buried into his shoulders, and it was with him that I burst into tears for the first time. Like me, he could not fathom that François could be having an affair. Unlike many other advisers, Pierre-René was always considerate. Over the past two years – or close enough – he had often had to put up with François' bouts of spectacular bad mood. In the evening I was the one who had to be a lightning rod. We would back each other up.

We exchanged a few words. I told him I was prepared to forgive François. I later learned that the idea of a separation statement had already been raised in that first meeting. My fate was sealed, but I did not know it yet.

Back to the room. A long, sleepless night was starting – insomnia had found a bed for the night. The same questions tormenting me – on repeat. François swallowed a sleeping pill to escape from that particular hell and slept for a few hours on the other side of the bed. I caught barely an hour's sleep and got up around 5 a.m. to watch the news channels in the living room. I snacked on cold leftovers from dinner – they were still out on the coffee table – and tuned into the radio channels. The 'information' had made the morning news headlines. Suddenly, it was all very real. Just one day earlier, everything had seemed almost fantastical.

François woke up. I was not going to be able to cope, I could tell. My resolve weakened – I did not want to hear any of it. I ran to the bathroom and took the little plastic bag hidden in a drawer among my beauty products. It contained sleeping pills – several sorts, tablets and sleeping syrup. François had followed me into the bathroom and tried to snatch the bag from me. I ran into the room. He caught the bag and it tore. Pills tumbled onto the bed and the floor. I managed to grab a few of them and swallowed what I could. All I wanted was to sleep – I could not bear to live through the next few hours. I could feel the hailstorm that was preparing to hit me and I wanted to batten down the hatches – I did not have the strength to withstand it. I wanted to escape one way or another. I passed out. That was the best I could have hoped for.

Was it daytime or night-time? What had happened? I sensed someone was trying to wake me. I had no idea how long I had slept. I would later find out that it was late morning. As if through a bank of fog, I could see the faces of two of my best friends, Brigitte and François Bachy, hovering above me. Brigitte explained that I could be hospitalised, that she had packed a suitcase for me. Two doctors were waiting in the next room. The health adviser to the Élysée had taken things in hand and called the professor who headed the psychiatry ward at the Pitié-Salpêtrière hospital. Both doctors asked me whether I would agree to be hospitalised. What were my options? I needed to be shielded from the storm – at that point I hardly knew who I was or what was going on. I could not manage alone.

I asked to see François before I left but one of the doctors was against it. I mustered the strength to say that I would not leave without seeing him… Someone went to get him. Seeing him gave me another shock. My legs failed me and I fell to the ground. Seeing him reminded me of his betrayal. It hurt me even more than the day before. Things were starting to speed up around me. It was immediately decided that I would be taken away. I could not stand up. Two security guards stood on either side of me and hoisted me up under the arms and held me up as best they could. The stairs seemed never-ending. Brigitte followed with my bag – a lovely bag given to me for my birthday by the team that worked with me at the Élysée, to use on official trips. But the pomp and ceremony of receptions was a long way away. The First Lady – unable to stand up or walk straight – looked like a rag doll that had been pulled apart. Brigitte rode with me in the car. I did not say a word during the entire trip. I simply could not talk.

I was admitted as soon as I arrived, and in no time I was settled into a hospital bed. What nightmare scenario had led me to this? A drip in my arm. A nightgown courtesy of the welfare services. Sedated into deep sleep. For how long? A day? Two days? I hardly knew, I had lost all concept of time. My first instinct when I woke up was to reach for both of my mobile phones. They were nowhere to be found. The doctor explained that they had been confiscated to 'protect' me from the 'outside world'. I demanded them back, threatening to leave. The doctors agreed to hand them back to me when they saw how determined I was.

The security guard who had been with me since the President's election took up headquarters in my room, wearing white scrubs. To keep a low profile, he sat in a chair near the door, dressed up as a nurse. He was the one who watched over the visits – as well as ensuring that only authorised visitors came through. Visits were rare. Everything was being controlled – but not by me, and I was not aware of it yet. A personal affair was being treated like a state affair. I was now no more than a file.

I confirmed to a journalist that I was in hospital. I had the feeling that something was going on at the Élysée. My intuition was vindicated. As soon as the news spread, 'they' wanted to get me out. The First Lady in hospital was not good for the President's image. Not much in the whole sorry affair was good for his image. Least of all the picture of him on the rue du Cirque with his motorbike helmet on his head. This time I stood my ground and told the doctor I wanted to stay a couple more days. Where would I have gone? Back to the rue Cauchy, to my flat – our flat? I was so drugged that I could not stand up; my blood pressure had dropped to 60. One day it dropped so low that the nurses were unable to take it.

The doctors were talking about sending me to a clinic to rest. My memories are vague. I remember the nurses coming to take my blood pressure very regularly, even waking me up during the night. I do not remember all of the visits, but I remember of course that my sons visited every day and brought me flowers and chocolates – as did my mother, who had rushed to my bedside from her small home town. I remember that François Bachy, my best friend, came every day too. Brigitte, meanwhile, was the link with the Élysée. She later told me that she had been astounded by the inhumanity she had encountered. Like talking to a brick wall, she said.

On day five, François had yet to visit, although he sent me fairly laconic daily messages. I learned that the doctors had forbidden him from coming to see me. I did not understand this decision, which, on top of being hurtful for me, was disastrous politically speaking. After a heated discussion, one of the doctors gave in and lifted the ban. He allowed a ten-minute visit. It lasted over an hour.

Again, my recollections are vague. The discussion

was calm. It could not have gone any other way given the astronomic dose of tranquilisers I was being fed. The head of the ward visited every ten minutes to make sure it was going well, then left again. He later told one of his friends it had felt like witnessing two lovers reuniting.

All I can recall is telling François I would go to his New Year Wishes event in Tulle – planned for that week. François was the elected representative of that little town and I had not missed a single one of his speeches there in years. Well before he became President, I went with him to hear his speech. It was our ritual – one the citizens of Tulle had come to expect, too. Just like our own election-day ritual. I have lost count of the number of times I canvassed the polling stations alongside him, all those times where we would end up in the cellar of La Guenne town hall drinking Roger's excellent wine and devouring his *crêpes* filled with rillettes.

Unsurprisingly, the answer was no. At first François tried to dissuade me with talk of my condition and eventually settled the matter by saying it was impossible on a political level. In short, he did not want me there. Even though I myself was prepared to face the stares from curious bystanders and ill-wishers alike.

Three months after I came out of hospital, I woke up in tears. Being apart from him on 24 March – the first day of the first round of the 2014 municipal elections – was very painful. Election dates brought back memories of utterly unique moments: it gave me such joy to experience the thrills of each election with him, as well as the annual Socialist Party summer conference in La Rochelle.

We were together for all of the major dates on the political calendar for over twenty years. I was there with him first as a journalist and then as his partner. We shared all the defining moments of his public life. They were intense moments. And with each year that passed the two of us were increasingly close – until the day everything changed, until the day we got together as a couple.

It was all over now. He no longer wanted me there. I was adamant: 'I will go. I'll drive there in my own car.' I have lost count of the number of times I drove down alone – by day or by night. I would not bat an eyelid at the thought of a five-hour drive for a stolen moment of intimacy – before driving all the way back up the A19 motorway. True passion is uniquely intoxicating.

The next day, in a state of extreme exhaustion, I was completely out of it. The day after that – for the President's New Year Wishes in Tulle – I took a turn for the worse. I could simply not get up. I tried to get out of bed but immediately collapsed. The Labour Minister's wife, Valérie, came to have lunch with me. She had a sandwich while I had the usual hospital tray. I could hardly hold my fork, let alone keep a conversation going. I struggled to stay awake and make the most of her visit. But it was a losing battle. I stopped fighting it. She let me rest.

My blood pressure had reached new lows. It was only later that I found out why: I was being heavily sedated to stop me from going to Tulle. My veins could not cope with the overdose.

The doctor was worried about me getting behind the wheel. He kept saying: 'You won't even make it to the end of the corridor!' I argued with him several times. Each time, espresso was the bargaining tool. He was the only one who made good coffee and allowed me to drink my daily dose – provided I made a few concessions.

True, he was a bit of an ogre, but I was rather fond of him. I appreciated his frankness and sensed that the whole affair made him slightly uneasy. He later told me he had been to the Élysée to keep the President informed of my condition. I do not know how much they discussed and whether that is when they decided on the 'anti-Tulle' operation.

I felt listless, the time passed without my noticing. The supportive nurses tried to shake me out of my misery. Everything was difficult: getting up, taking a shower, brushing my hair. They nudged me: 'Don't let yourself go!' They had always seen me as a First Lady who took care of her appearance; now they were faced with a wreck who would not even bother changing her pyjamas. They let me know they were behind me – beyond their professional obligations.

My release date came around. I was to continue my convalescence at La Lanterne – formerly a residence for the Prime Minister, it was made available to the President in 2007. It is a peaceful place, adjacent to the Park of Versailles.

Every minute detail of the exit operation had been planned to avoid the paparazzi. It was like a covert ops evacuation. I struggled to put one foot in front of the other. I held onto a security guard's arm, swaying slightly. Obviously we avoided the front door. The security routine was stepped up. The car we normally used was turned into a decoy and sent out first on a scouting mission.

The trick worked. Television crews and photographers were stationed in front of La Lanterne but they only caught the fleeting image of a car with stained glass windows pulling into the driveway, nothing more. They did not even glimpse my shadow. The word is apt: I was a mere shadow of my former self.

Being back in a place I loved felt good – it was there that I had my fondest memories of moments shared with the President. A peaceful harbour of a house with its high windows that bathed the rooms in light. A property protected by tall trees that have been there for centuries. I was welcomed by the caretakers who have been managing the property for twenty-five years – guardian angels, really. The couple had seen many a prime minister – before Nicolas Sarkozy snatched back this little slice of paradise for the presidency. They have witnessed many a secret meeting, many a family celebration and have no doubt seen their fair share of drama. But they keep it to themselves. They have never betrayed anyone, never spilled the slightest detail. I used to enjoy having coffee with them in the morning, we would talk about this and that. We always shared pleasant moments. They saw how lonely I was.

One of the young Élysée doctors was posted in the next-door room 24/7, monitoring my blood pressure and feeding me a treatment of anti-anxiety meds and sedatives. I felt light-headed as soon as I tried to get up and had to sit back down immediately. One morning I only just managed to catch myself before falling. I was very cautious after that.

Every day a friend came to visit. As did my family. They did not tell me everything that was going on in the outside world. They protected me from the mob, the insane speculation and the scandal-mongering newspaper and magazine covers. One day, my mother, my son and I were walking around the garden to make the most of a bit of sunshine – far from suspecting that some paparazzi had gone to the lengths of hiding in the trees. They could only photograph us from behind, which did not stop a gossip magazine from purchasing one of the pictures. The media machine was at full throttle. It gobbled up every unimportant piece of my life.

The previous summer I had often gone alone to La Lanterne while François was working in Paris. I felt sheltered there, and got into the habit of going on long bicycle rides. My security guards and I felt like we were not far off from going pro. Every day we would cycle 37 km through the park and the forest of Versailles. We timed ourselves, hoping to improve, to shave off a few minutes and increase our kilometre/hour ratio. Nothing could stop us, not even a rainy day. It was a pleasure I did not tire of.

François joined me mid-August. He had finally allowed himself a few days off – sort of. He barely looked up from his files and refused to leave the grounds of La Lanterne. Going for a stroll meant no more than a couple of walks around the garden. That did not stop me from going on my bicycle rides. The paparazzi were everywhere. All around the park. In fact, a picture of me on my bike had been published in *Le Parisien* a few days earlier.

One morning, as we were nearing a sharp bend around the park's cross-shaped Grand Canal, I spotted two photographers and headed towards them without warning the two policemen who were escorting me. The paparazzi had made a day of it: they had thought of everything, down to a blanket and a cool box. One of the paparazzi got scared and lifted his hands in the air as if I had been holding a gun: 'We didn't take the photo in *Le Parisien*, we swear! It wasn't us! Really it wasn't.'

I was amused by how terrified they looked.

'That's not why I'm here, I came to tell you that you are wasting your time. The President will not come out, you won't get any pictures of him. You can photograph me on my bike every day but what's the point? You won't get *him*. You'd be better off spending time with your families.'

Predictably, they did not believe me and, just as predictably, they wasted their time 'shooting' me every morning – hands on the handlebar, no hands... Still, remembering that photographer's panic always makes me smile, just as I smile at the memory of my security guard's playful comment: 'Well, you definitely don't need *us*!'

Last January those oddly happy memories suddenly seemed very distant. I tried to do a bit of indoor cycling, but had to give up straight away – I did not have the strength for it. I stayed in bed. The days passed aimlessly, flicking through old magazines – I avoided current news like the plague – listening to music and sleeping. Every day I received dozens of anonymous letters – they were addressed to the Élysée, which couriered them over. Some letters moved me to tears. Many women – but not just women – wanted to express their support. I put a few letters to one side, promising myself I would write back and I did manage a few thank you letters.

A week went by that way. I had lost all concept of time. Time was suspended, medicated, anaesthetised. While the worldwide media machine printed pictures of me, discussed my life, my fate, I avoided reading magazines at all costs. I only read the countless emails and text messages that had come in while I was in hospital. From friends I had not seen in a long time, from distant family, work relations, writers, people who had found my number even though I did not know them. I also received messages from women I had helped through their bereavement or their troubles – women who, in turn, wanted to comfort me. I was particularly touched by a message from Eva Sandler, who had lost her husband and her two little boys in the Toulouse school shooting. I had no right to complain – I was going through an ordeal, not a tragedy.

From the Élysée, I only received three messages sent by advisers. The rest of them had gone into hiding. I was already being treated like a pariah. Within the government, only four ministers dared send me a kind word.

Those I knew best went AWOL. Their deafening silence was highlighted by the messages from the 'other side' – from Claude Chirac, Carla Bruni-Sarkozy, Cécilia Attias,[1] Jean-Luc Mélenchon, Alain Delon and many more. In politics, it is best not to be on the losing side.

In under a week, not only did my life explode but I was given evidence of the extent of cynicism in the small world of politics – friends, advisers and courtesans.

François announced that he would visit the following Saturday 'to talk'. Shortly before dinnertime, he said. When he arrived we went through to the big living room, the one we call the music room, where an imposing grand piano sits. It is not the original instrument but it *is* in that room that André Malraux's wife sat down to play when Charles de Gaulle's Minister for Culture lived there. The General had been greatly saddened by Malraux's tragedy – the death of both of his children in an accident. De Gaulle had granted André Malraux the privilege of isolating himself there with his wife and her son. Every weekend, as if in a bid to numb himself, Malraux tackled the interior decoration of La Lanterne. Namely, he turned the old stables into his library.

François and I sat opposite one another, on different sofas. The atmosphere was heavy, the distance between us was already palpable. It was then that he mentioned separating. I could not understand his logic. He was the

---

1  Formerly Cécilia Sarkozy.

one caught red-handed and I was the one to pay the price. But so it went. His decision did not seem irrevocable, not yet, but I did not have the strength to argue. He tried not to be too heartless but he had delivered a harsh sentence. It did not really register; it was as if I was under anaesthetic.

We moved to the dining room for dinner. With the butlers there, the conversation turned to banal matters. We went to bed – in separate bedrooms. We had never done that. He wanted to mark the end. I had a fitful night, peopled with nightmares and hallucinations caused by the medication.

I woke with a start, convinced there was someone in the room. I thought of François wrapping another woman in his arms. Who made the first move? What did he tell her about us? What was he looking for in her that I could not give him? Imagining it was painful. I tried to push the images to the back of my mind but they kept surfacing, again and again. I was drowning in those images, choked up with tears.

In the morning, François told me he would leave after lunch and that two of my very close friends, Constance and Valérie, wanted to come and see me. Why weren't they calling me themselves? I wanted to be alone, to find myself and understand what was happening.

François was insistent. He did not feel comfortable

leaving me alone with my despair when he was about to go and meet his mistress. I did not know that my two friends had arrived in Versailles that morning. He had cooked up this strategy to ease his conscience – he was not leaving me by myself. They were waiting in a café for his green light to come to La Lanterne. He wanted to pass the baton on to them. They bombarded me with messages begging me to let them come over. I gave in and that was all to the good. Their presence was comforting after François had left.

The two of us had planned to see each other again the following Thursday. Thursday had always been our day. The day we started our relationship. The day we met every week between 2005 and 2007. The day Joe Dassin famously sang about. We listened to that song countless times in my car, on repeat. We would sing along: 'Remember? It was a Thursday / A big day / A big step towards true love.'

I decided we would meet in our home, in the rue Cauchy. We would be alone there and could speak freely. He arrived on time, which was unusual for him. He had brought lunch prepared by the Élysée in a big white metal lunchbox, with ready-made platters that just needed to be microwaved.

His security guards stayed outside the building. Since *Closer* had printed pictures of one of them bringing croissants – bright and early – to the flat François and Julie Gayet used, the security guards knew better than to cross paths with me.

We set the table like an ordinary couple, but we weren't hungry. It all seemed unreal. At the end of the meal it was as if nothing had changed: he got up and made some coffee, then he laid it out in the living room. It was time to discuss some important issues.

I wanted the ground to open up and swallow me whole. I was scared of the unknown, of what would happen after we separated – not least financially. I shared my concerns with François. Since the divorce from the father of my children, the financial burden of my three boys was 100 per cent my responsibility. It was the price I had to pay for my freedom – to be with François. At the time, I had not hesitated. I had also decided to keep the name Trierweiler, my pen name for over fifteen years. I wanted to bear the same name as my children. I was divorcing their father; I did not want to feel like I was separating from them.

François knew that I could not manage alone on my *Paris-Match* salary. There was the rent of our flat on the rue Cauchy and my children's expenses – their accommodation and their studies. When we took on the rental, I had income from both *Paris-Match* and TV – I had been working with Direct 8 (now called D8) since the channel launched in 2005.

Once he became President, François demanded that I give up television. I had been in talks with the channel's executives about launching a new humanitarian show that would be compatible with my role as a First Lady. We had planned to make a series of documentaries featuring me interviewing celebrities on themes of general interest: girls' education around the world, water protection, refugees. For each programme I would have travelled to two or three countries.

I was very excited about this project, which was well on its way. But the French authorities had just greenlit the purchase of Direct 8 by Canal+. Some journalists had complained that there was a conflict of interest there. One sunny Sunday in September at La Lanterne he ordered: 'You have to give up TV!'

His curt tone was not one that left any room for negotiation and I agreed immediately. There had been the 'tweet business' and Ségolène Royal's electoral defeat in the spring. I did not want any more arguments and problems between us. But by giving up that day, I had lost two-thirds of my income and he knew that.

Money has never been what drives me, but I have always had an almost visceral fear of what lies in store. I am afraid of being in a position of instability. I am worried I will not have a roof over my head when I am too old to work. I know that one of my grandmothers was utterly destitute when she died. I have always been independent. I remember my mother, before she found a job as a cashier, was forced to 'ask' my father for money – out of his meagre invalidity pension. As a child, I viewed these scenes as a humiliation, a complete deprivation of freedom.

I built my identity around the rejection of a single thing: I would never be financially dependent on someone. Not once in my life have I ever asked anyone for money, least of all a man. I have not forgotten the time my mother realised in a supermarket that she had lost her wallet. I remember her panic: she was wondering how she would feed us over the following days. I cannot remember how old I was at the time but her expression of despair has always stayed with me.

I come from a family that does not believe in overdrafts. In my family, you don't spend money you don't have and we are still attentive to the price of things. It is how we live. I was shaped by that upbringing and it is still part of who I am: I do not know how to 'go all out' and 'splurge'. I always use the example of a day I was shopping in the sales with a friend, at a factory outlet. I was buying clothes for my sons and the sales assistant mistakenly greeted me with an 'Oh, Mrs Sarkozy!' that made me smile. I waved my hand to tell her she was mistaken. She corrected herself – 'Oh, yes, you are Hollande's wife' – and I heard a couple buying clothes just in front of me comment that 'if even wives of presidents come and do their shopping here, then we really are in a crisis!'

On another sales day – what can I say, the leopard does not change its spots – I bought a pair of trainers for one of my sons. The sales assistant recognised me and said: 'So here you are living at the Élysée Palace and you work too?'

'Sir, how would I pay for these trainers if I did not earn a living?'

He understood and took my credit card with a smile.

Though I agreed to give up my TV show for François, I was adamant that I would keep my job at *Paris-Match*. I could not begin to imagine no longer having a job or a salary. I was the French President's partner, I had an office in the Élysée, just like the other First Ladies before me. It was an entirely voluntary function, heading a small team of official representatives dedicated to humanitarian and social work. Why on earth should I have given up my job and income? Why should I have been the only woman in France who wasn't allowed to work?

When we made our relationship public in 2007 I had already given up the politics column of *Paris-Match* two years earlier, in favour of the cultural pages where there was no conflict of interest. How could the fact that I was writing about novels possibly bother anyone?

Over the past eight years I have never once claimed to be a literary critic. I merely tried to give *Paris-Match* readers a taste for literature. I tried to convey my own reader's sensibility. Books opened up new horizons and endless possibilities for me. Without literature I would never have become the woman I am today. I have loved reading ever since I first learned to decipher words. As a child I would spend hours in public libraries. My mother had got into the habit of leaving my sister and me there while she did the shopping, because when we were surrounded by books we were happy.

The unmistakable dusty smell of books that have been on the shelves for aeons is my own personal madeleine de Proust. For me, *that* is the perfume of childhood.

When my big sister Pascale – I was six at the time – was in charge of 'running errands' she would hide away a couple of francs to buy me those flimsy little books that were worth next to nothing. Growing up, I literally read everything and *any*thing. I had no one to guide me.

Like many French families, my parents had taken out a *France-Loisirs* book subscription. Every quarter, a new book was sent to our house. I read, dreamt, learned. Since my thirteenth birthday I had kept a notebook in which I jotted down the titles of the books I read. As I flicked through the first pages of my notebook, I remembered that pick 'n' mix of classic novels and run-of-the-mill books – though many of them have not stood the test of time, I read everything that was sent to me.

I always asked for books at Christmas – I could not imagine a better present. The books I got for Christmas were mine to keep, I did not have to give them back to the library.

Through my work for the culture pages I received dozens of books every week. I still felt the same emotion every time I opened the large envelopes the editors sent me and discovered the book that was hidden inside. There were so many that I lost my proprietorial instinct. I gave the Fleury-Mérogis prison for women 95 per cent of the books I received.

It was a real joy to write my book column for *Paris-Match* every week or so. It was even more precious than the time I spent at the Élysée. I saw it as a victory over all the people who denied me the right to work, as well as a personal victory. Had I not been forced to prepare for my column, I would no doubt have allowed myself to get caught up in a whirlwind of meetings, trips and receptions without ever opening a single book. How sad! Powering up my computer, finding myself alone with my thoughts in front of the blank page, disconnecting from the world, concentrating, helped me get past many a hurdle.

Just not this one.

It was a dark day, a Thursday, when François left me. I

was in no state to focus on more than a couple of lines in a novel. I stood by, helpless, and watched our relationship unravel. The President assured me that I had nothing to worry about – I would no doubt receive job offers that would help me get back on my feet.

After discussing the financial side of things, François brought up all the points that concerned him. He wanted me to give up on the idea of writing a book, an idea I had been toying with for a few days and one I had shared with him.

Being made to give up anything that belonged to 'my life after him' was absolutely out of the question. He insisted that we should announce 'our' separation in a joint statement. I refused. I did not want that separation. There was nothing 'joint' about it. He was forcing it on me. The tone of the discussion was calm and cold.

It was all so sad.

Before he left, I demanded he return his key.

'You are throwing me out of your life, this is not your home anymore, I want the key. I want to be free to invite whomever I want whenever I want.'

I knew he would not like hearing that. He had been cheating on me for over a year but could not stand the idea of me living my own life. Men are like that. He tried to argue.

'I'll have it sent over to you.'

'No, I want it back now.'

François called the security guard who had the key and met him in the corridor. He came back with the key but he needed it to go down to the basement where the car was parked – the building was secured and you couldn't get to the car park without using the key in the lift.

Not a problem. I decided to go down to the underground car park with them to get the key back immediately. There we were, François and I going down six floors in the company of the croissant courier – the policeman who had been immortalised by the paparazzi. 'So you didn't bring croissants today?' I asked, looking him in the eye. 'Is that what you think your job as a policeman is? I can't even begin to understand how you can still be here.'

He looked down at his shoes and said nothing. His eyes filled with tears. François did not say a word.

I went straight to La Lanterne. It had been agreed that I would stay in Versailles until Saturday, the day before my trip to India. I had made a commitment with *Action contre la Faim*[2] several months ago. We were supposed to push on to Madhya Pradesh, several hours' drive from the airport, down chaotic and dangerous roads, but I agreed to cut the trip short because I wasn't sure I was physically sound and strong enough to cope.

---

2   Action Against Hunger.

For days, everyone had been trying to make me give up the trip. The President was more insistent than most. But it was not my health he was worried about. In his mind there was no longer a First Lady. (It begs the question: was there ever one?) What mattered to him was that I kept my mouth shut.

I had a few days to rest in La Lanterne before my trip. I was not looking forward to spending the last evening, Friday evening, alone with my sorrow. I had invited several close friends over for dinner, as if to prove to myself that life would go on. They all came to wrap me up in their friendship. What would I have become without my friends? We spent a hearty, joyous evening. I had asked the doctor permission not to take my medicine so that I could drink a couple glasses of wine. I did not get much sleep that night.

On Saturday I had planned to meet François late afternoon to agree on the statement. Three of my friends stayed the night. I emptied my things, gathered the summer clothes that I kept at La Lanterne, my books and a few personal belongings. My friends helped me. After a quick and simple meal, it was time to go. I went to say goodbye to the caretaker couple, Josyane and Éric: 'So … I just wanted to say that this is the last time we will be seeing each other.'

They protested – they thought I was joking.

In a broken voice I answered: 'The President and I are separating, it will be announced this evening.'

It was their turn to show their emotion. With tears in their eyes they took me in their arms and cajoled me with words of comfort. I cried with them. I will never forget that moment. Ever. Nor will I forget saying goodbye to the two cooks who came into work that day. When they started crying too I had to excuse myself: 'I'm sorry, I'm not going to be able to hold it in.'

I could no longer hold back the tears. I wanted to leave with dignity but those demonstrations of affection moved me very deeply and I had to save some strength for what awaited me. I dived into the waiting car. The TV cameras were already there, on the prowl. The journalists were waiting outside the gate on their motorbikes, ready to follow my every move as if to witness my public execution.

Our first stop was rue Cauchy – our home, which would now be only mine – followed by hordes of photographers and cameramen. We went in through the underground car park to avoid pictures. To avoid being followed all the way to the Élysée, a strategy was needed – not one but two decoy cars were used. By the time we left, the hounds were long gone. One of the cars had even gone back to La Lanterne, dragging behind it part of the press. I managed to smile about that.

I am not sure what went through my mind as I entered the Élysée gardens through the Marigny gate. I had made a habit of always coming into the Élysée Palace through that discreet entrance rather than through the ceremonial courtyard. I never really allowed myself to go in through the ceremonial courtyard. It was as if, deep down, I had always felt illegitimate. Yet I lived there for twenty months with the President – whose life I was *officially* sharing.

On Saturday 25 January 2014, my heart sank. This time it was the end. When I arrived in the private apartment, I started to put together the outfits I would need for India, then I sent François a text to let him know I was there. Like the last time, there was tension in the air – each of us sat at our usual place in the living room. Again, he pushed for a joint statement. Again, I refused – sticking to the same arguments. We replayed our previous scene.

Again, he asked me to give up on my trip to India: 'You'll get all the journalists.'

He was preparing to dismiss me and the only thing that mattered to him was that the press should follow him, rather than me.

'So what? Maybe I will get more than you got in Turkey.'

It was a pathetic attempt but I was trying to provoke him. He was worried about what I would say to the press. I said I had not yet decided.

Squirming uneasily in his seat, he read me the separation statement he had planned to hand in to the AFP. Eighteen cold and proud words on a small piece of paper, each of them like a stab in the heart. I crumpled at the harshness of the phrasing, at the contempt with which he 'made it known' that he was 'putting an end' to his 'shared life with Valérie Trierweiler'…

I stood up and left screaming: 'Go on then! Send your bloody statement out if that's what you want.'

He tried to stop me, to wrap me in his arms: 'We can't say goodbye this way. Kiss me.'

He even suggested we spend the last night together… I tore myself from his arms forcefully and left without turning back, tears streaming down my face.

I would later learn that it took three official advisers to draft my statement renouncing our relationship. The death certificate of our love, sandwiched between two piles of current affairs that needed to be dealt with speedily.

We are not always in control of our emotions. The two of us fell in love when we were not free. It was not a meaningless affair. What was going on now? Why was he acting with such inhumanity? Such violence? Tenderness was apparently not an option; he could at least have shown some consideration for me.

I had to meet my security guards who were waiting

for me in the car. I was in floods of tears and tried to hide behind a tree so they would not see me in that state. One of the butlers kindly handed me a handkerchief. I was the handkerchief that had just been thrown out a second before.

I did my best to grin and bear it and joined the team. All I could say was that we were going back to the rue Cauchy. No one dared say a word. We had just crossed the Alexandre III bridge when I received a message from my executioner. He had just released the guillotine and was sending me a love note: 'I want your forgiveness because I still love you.'

All it achieved was that I started crying even more. Why was he doing this? Was he being sincere or was it just further evidence of his cowardice?

It took us a little while to get back to the rue Cauchy flat. Alexandre, my security guard, followed me up in the lift. Seeing me in such a state made him as miserable as me.

He was worried about me and asked me if I was going to pull through.

'Yes, I'll be all right,' I said.

Avoid switching on the television or the radio no matter what. My phone kept beeping with messages. I barely looked at them. The news was spreading like wildfire. Just as – when I was in hospital – I had not seen the magazine covers in the international press after the scooter pictures were published, now I was not aware that the news of our separation was going around the world already. I did not want to hear it; I needed to protect myself from this media storm.

It wasn't the first storm I had weathered but it was the worst of them all and I was not very strong. I rifled through my DVD collection. There was only one thing I wanted: to get into bed and take my mind elsewhere. Anywhere as long as it was far away from reality.

I picked *Sarah's Key* as I had wanted to watch the film adaptation of Tatiana de Rosnay's novel for a long time. It tells the story of a US journalist who pieces together the life of little Sarah, arrested as part of the Vel d'Hiv Round-Up.[3]

It was barely 8 p.m. and I was under the duvet with no inclination whatsoever to eat dinner. I watched the film with my laptop on my knees. I shut the world out, unsure whether I was crying over the sadness in the film or over my own life. By the time the credits rolled I was completely drained. That evening, I truly understood the meaning of the expression 'crying your eyes out'.

Like a trapped bee bumping against a windowpane, the same thoughts went back and forth in my head.

---

3   A raid and mass arrest of Jews in Paris conducted by the Nazis in July 1942.

How could he have done this to me? If we still loved each other, how had we reached this point? I reminded myself that the following day I would be on my way to India – I held on to that thought like a drowning person clinging to a raft.

So how *had* we reached this point?

How had we become so distant in such a short space of time? Power was like acid, it ate away at our love from the inside. The Gayet rumour had been poisoning my life since October 2012.

It was around that time, five months after the presidential election, that I heard it for the first time. Having myself been the butt of so many abject rumours, I did not believe it for a second. But then I heard that a dinner with artists had taken place at the Élysée Palace a few days earlier, on a Saturday evening. I had not been informed that it was being organised and I had certainly not been invited. Not a single person told me about it. Not François, nor his team – which was supposed to liaise with mine and coordinate agendas when he had time to himself – nor the President's cultural adviser, who had suggested the dinner in the first place.

That Saturday I was stuck in Isle-Adam. For years I had rented a house in that little town outside of Paris to be with my children part of the week – back when my ex-husband and I had shared custody. As my children had now all moved to Paris I no longer had a reason to keep the house. So I boxed up my things. My sons helped me during the day and went out to meet their friends in the evening. It was my last weekend there.

It never even occurred to me to ask François to help me. He was the President and he had other things to do. I sorted through everything and, as was the case with each move, it was an opportunity to relive some defining moments. What should I do with my collection of *Paris-Match* magazines? I couldn't keep them all. I flicked through a few of them. One of the magazines captured my attention. It was a 1992 issue, France was in the middle of an economic and political crisis and François Mitterrand was on the cover. Édith Cresson was Prime Minister and the situation was catastrophic. 'Meanwhile Mitterrand is playing golf, ambling down the quays and browsing for books.' That was the caption of the article. It wasn't an attack, quite the opposite – the journalist was praising the President for being able to keep a cool head and gain some perspective. How things have changed! Nowadays nothing goes – not even a fortnight's holiday in Fort de Brégançon after a year and a half spent campaigning. Different times... In 2012, the press was up in arms about François' tanned face and our outings on the beach when half of France was on holiday. Twenty years earlier, France had looked on in wonderment at a President who could play golf in the midst of political turmoil.

I looked at a few more pictures. Pictures of my children when they were little, pictures of a life that was flying by at high speed. François called me around 11 p.m. but did not mention the dinner that he and Julie Gayet had just attended.

Obviously I thought it was strange that I had been excluded from this dinner at the Élysée but I didn't let it alarm me. A month later, in November 2012, the rumour came back with a vengeance. Paris was alive with the news of a picture which apparently proved the affair. I grilled François: had he taken the actress home after dinner? He assured me he had not.

The whispers around town were starting to become chatter. The AFP was on the trail. One detail emerged: it seemed that it was a picture of him on the rue du Faubourg Saint-Honoré, where she lived at the time, a stone's throw from the Élysée Palace. I called François from my office. 'I'm on my way,' he said. In less than a minute he was there. We went into the library next to my office. He told me he had been to her flat in September but for a meeting with other artists.

'How many of you were there?'

'I can't remember, ten, a dozen.'

'That's impossible, you're lying, it would have been

in your diary. A President does not do that sort of thing unscheduled.'

I got angry. Under pressure, he told me that Julie Gayet had hosted a dinner with Pinault, the influential businessman, so that the two of them could meet. He did not specify whether it was the father or the son but he knew both of them and no President needs a matchmaker. In fact, I distinctly remembered him telling me one evening that he had had a *tête-à-tête* dinner at Pinault's flat.

He had not come home late, we had met at the rue Cauchy and he told me that the businessman planned to return two Chinese statuettes that had been looted from the Beijing Summer Palace in 1860 by the Franco-British troops. Two bronze animal heads, a rat and a dog, that were missing from a twelve-piece set – a restitution of the Chinese calendar. This restitution was to be added to the Franco-Chinese diplomatic programme for the upcoming state visit in April. What had Julie Gayet got to do with that? Why had I been cast aside yet again?

The lie grated. But still I did not believe he was having an affair with her. In my mind, François was too invested in his role to take such a risk. And I had the weakness of trusting that we loved each other enough for that not to happen. Was I being naive? One of my journalist friends explained that right-wing policemen were fuelling the rumour. He suspected a political group of trying to create instability by fabricating stories to suit its purpose, as this was frequent practice. It was also my feeling.

I had been the victim of methods such as those during the presidential campaign: a false police record was circulated around press editorial boards. My lawyer had called an emergency meeting. Journalists from *L'Express* also contacted me to discuss it before the story ran. They knew the document was a fake and wanted to condemn the tactics used by the 'other side'. If the file was to be believed, I had had affairs with half of the political establishment – right-wing and left-wing alike.

The document was a shoddy fake, but I had felt completely undermined by the whole sordid business. The only thing that mattered to me was that my children should not think that their mother was that sort of woman. For me, it was the first media tsunami – the first in a long series.

When the weekly issue of *L'Express* came out, my telephone started ringing off the hook. It was the press, of course – political affiliation did not matter in this instance, they were all calling. I did not pick up. I needed to protect myself. I did not switch on the television. I sought refuge in my Isle-Adam home. My eldest son called me: 'What have you done, Mum? Why are they talking about you everywhere?'

'Nothing, I haven't done anything. Except being a candidate's partner, which makes me a target.'

I had immediately gone home, put a load in the washing machine, as if to clean all that muck off. The list was so grotesque that it had made François smile. It did not make me smile.

Having experienced falsities myself, I did not believe the Gayet rumour. Seduction, quite possibly, but not infidelity. I reminded François of his lie several times – that dinner she attended when I was not invited. Then the rumour started to die out.

It was a short-lived respite. I was waiting for François in the Élysée Hall of Honour before an official trip to Russia, late February 2013. He was running late. I was told that a famous paparazzo was in his office. It seemed very odd. I took the stairs of the beautiful Murat staircase four by four – a staircase I hardly ever used – and walked past the ushers with determination. Under normal circumstances I would never dare barge into François' office; in the last twenty months I had only been in five times. I opened the imposing door without knocking and addressed the unwelcome guest: 'What do you think you are doing here? The likes of you have no place here.'

I knew him well, we were even friends at one point at *Paris-Match*, until it became apparent that he was not reliable.

He replied that he was here to warn François about all the rumours that were circulating. I decided to make

the first move: 'They say he has a black child in Corrèze.
You mean the Gayet rumour? We've heard that one, it's
been going around Paris, we don't need you for that one.'
Then I addressed François: 'We have to go, everyone is
waiting for you.' After which I put my arm through his
and turned on my heels, leaving the paparazzo behind.

The atmosphere in the car on the way to Orly airport
was very tense. 'What did he want?' I asked.

'Nothing special, just to inform me of all the rumours.'

For the first time, I was suspicious: 'You wouldn't have
agreed to see him at the last minute if you didn't have a
guilty conscience.'

'Believe me, that's not the case,' he replied.

There were policemen in the car so I was forced to
leave it at that.

A month later the rumour emerged again. It was
the same scenario. It seemed that pictures were doing the
rounds. I was also told that Julie Gayet was doing nothing to deny the story; on the contrary, she appeared to be
playing the mystery card. I decided to call her. It was 28
March 2013 and that very evening François was making
a television appearance. My phone call did not seem to
surprise her. I explained that the rumour was very trying
for me and harmful for François politically speaking. She
replied that it was equally unpleasant for her. I suggested
she deny it and put an end to this unpleasant episode.

She agreed. I then sent another message to suggest waiting until the next day, so as not to pollute the presidential interview. 'I'm afraid it might be too late, my lawyer has already sent out the statement,' came her reply.

The timing was poor but the official statement denying the affair reassured me. The terms were unambiguous and firm. The actress announced that she would sue anyone who peddled the hypothesis of an affair. The wool was pulled over my eyes. I don't understand how people can lie so effortlessly.

In any case it gave us a momentary break. I relaxed for a while. Meanwhile, imperceptibly, François distanced himself. Was he really pulling away from me or was the cancer of jealousy playing tricks on me? The rumour came and went. One evening, I had it out with François: 'Swear to me on my son's life that it is not true and I won't bring it up again.'

He swore on my son's life and asked me to give this so-called story a rest. He had too much work and too many worries to bother with gossip. I was, he reckoned, starting to become tiresome with this 'hogwash'. I quote. Hogwash.

His self-assurance should have put my mind at rest for good but the poison had seeped in. I reasoned with myself and put his distance down to the pressures of his work. Everything was difficult for him, the political climate was not good. We were still a real couple, though, and we continued to share good times together.

The summer ended, autumn came around. The situation in France worsened. François' popularity ratings had plummeted. Then there was Canal+'s *Le Grand Journal*[4] news show on 16 December 2013. I did not watch the programme live and was unaware that Julie Gayet was one of the guests. I received a text message from a friend just before a dinner we had to go to: 'Have you watched TV this evening?'

'No, why?' I asked.

'You need to watch it.'

Before I could watch it, François came to pick me up at the flat and we left together for the dinner.

A journalist had suggested he meet 'real people'. As it happened, it was a gang of Parisian bohos in a beautiful apartment with a view onto a seventeenth-century paved courtyard. I caught the rerun of *Le Grand Journal* on the internet afterwards. One of the actors in Julie Gayet's latest film was adamant that the President had been on set. She did not deny it, she merely simpered.

I immediately called François on his mobile. He did not pick up. I tried getting through to him by calling his secretaries – something I did very rarely. I said it was

---

4  A French news and talk show airing every weekday evening on Canal+.

urgent and I needed to speak to him as soon as possible. They promised they would put him through right after his meeting. He called me back promptly. I did not beat around the bush: 'Did you go on the set of her film?'

He assured me he had not. But this time my patience had reached its limits. I was getting angry. He sensed it. I demanded a statement denying the affair. He promised it would be done within the hour. I left several messages on Julie Gayet's voicemail, asking her to call me back. Which she never did. When François asked me to, in 2006, I similarly ignored calls from Ségolène Royal – François' partner at the time. How ironic ... infidelity is an infernal cycle.

We met that evening for dinner. My youngest son still lived with us but was not home that evening. The two of us had dinner together in the living room. François spoke of this and that – carefully avoiding the subject. His evasiveness was unbearable. I cut to the chase and told him I did not understand that girl's attitude – refusing to dispel doubt – and reminded him that I had been beyond patient with this rumour. I expected him to take my side and fight back against her. But instead of reassuring me, he immediately leapt to Julie Gayet's defence. I was outraged by his reaction and felt humiliated. I was fuming, too much was being left unsaid, it drove me mad. We fought and he spat horrendous things at me.

I went to the bathroom and took all the remaining sleeping pills out of the pack. There must have been about eight. I returned to the living room and swallowed them in front of him. I did not know whether the story was true – I could hardly believe it – I simply could not understand his attitude. I could not stand his silence any longer.

He had become so cold, so different – indifferent, even – and I felt he did not love me anymore.

He tried to drag me to the bathroom to make me throw up. My actions had been a cry for help. I passed out on the sofa. It was as if I was in a coma: I could no longer feel my body, I could not talk, but I could hear. Except that all I heard was his silence. He did not say a word, he did not even utter my name. He straightened my legs, touched my forehead and left. I stayed alone. The doctor was not called… No one came. The Élysée is a beehive, the heart of power, but private apartments are like bubbles of silence, protected areas no one dares penetrate – hang your chaos at the door. At times I have felt desperately alone there.

I eventually managed to drag myself to the bedroom and got a few hours' sleep. I do not know whether he came back, whether he slept by my side. I cannot remember anything; the sleeping pills turned the lights out in my brain. I woke the next morning around midday. The

Christmas party we were hosting for the children of the Élysée was due to start at 2 p.m. I had been the one to organise it and I knew many of the underprivileged and disabled children attending – I could simply not let them down.

I wasn't sure whether I was fit to go. I got out of bed and stood up, feeling nauseous. I wanted to make it to the party at all costs. Besides, I firmly intended to shine in his eyes. I wanted him to see me, I wanted him to look at me at last. I decided not to wear the pink dress I had selected for the event, but opted instead for a Dior evening gown, adorned with rhinestones, that was on loan for a state dinner. The Élysée hairdresser and make-up girl arrived. Olivier and Nadia were nothing short of magicians.

'Today I would like to pull out all the stops.'

I have never worn jeans; I have always tried to exude a certain elegance – a timeless style. When I arrived at the Élysée Palace, it was a whole new story! I had started buying fashion magazines as a teenager, daydreaming about all the outfits I would never wear. When I worked in television a stylist brought me chic clothes but never haute couture. I did not even dare dream of it! I took my first steps as a First Lady in prêt-à-porter. Soon, very famous and respected haute couture designers offered to lend me outfits that were more suited to my role. I wore

Yves Saint Laurent, as well as a lot of Dior – I adored his dresses. Sometimes I went to the shop, and sometimes the outfits were brought to the Élysée for fittings that lasted for hours on end.

I still go to haute couture fashion shows.

The effect of the sleeping pills had not yet worn off so my voice was very calm – I felt like I was swaddled in cotton. The hairdresser and the make-up girl got down to work, giving it their all. We took our time. They transformed me. When I was ready I went downstairs, stopping by my office on the way.

My team gave me a warm welcome. We decided to take a picture all together. We posed several times, grinning widely. Not a single one of them could have imagined what had happened just one day earlier.

I had not seen François since he had abandoned me on the sofa. The plan was that I would attend the children's show alone; the President was only expected to make an appearance afterwards. Six hundred and fifty small faces had already taken their seats, and awaited the start of the show impatiently. The room was buzzing, filled with the sound of their laughter and their voices.

I stopped to give those I had already met a kiss. Most of them were in a wheelchair. When the singer, M. Pokora, arrived, the room went mad. At the end of the show, I was to join the President and return to the

event with him in tow. I waited for him at the bottom
of the Murat staircase in the Élysée. As soon as he laid
eyes on me I could tell that I had hit the nail on the
head with my outfit. 'You are breathtaking,' he said, 'you
look like a queen.'

We made our entrance together. For once he waited
for me – he had taken to walking one step ahead of me,
completely unconcerned about me. I went on stage with
him though it was unplanned. He said a few words to the
young public and, for the first time in months, he said a
few words of thanks to me – public thanks for organising
this enchanted Christmas.

Moments later I was dancing with a young man I did
not know. Afterwards François and I went from table
to table handing out gifts, posing for pictures and sign-
ing autographs. He was rather attentive to me. He came
with me to speak to various organisations when I asked
him to. The children could not get enough of us – they
wanted a photo with the President, one with me, then
one with both of us, and autographs too! An hour later,
François went back to work.

I stayed until the end – at 4 p.m. Angela Merkel was
expected an hour later and the staff had to pull off the
feat of putting the function room back in order in such
a short amount of time.

During that interval I saw Sarah and her children

Eva and Raphaël in my office. The children's father had died in Afghanistan in June 2012 – alongside three of his comrades-in-arms. After they died, I had accompanied François to the Invalides, to meet with the families. A tearful Sarah had asked the President for a special dispensation authorising a posthumous wedding – which he had of course granted. Her request had deeply moved me. I had travelled to the Pas-de-Calais department to deliver the document in person. Sarah managed a centre for disabled children, which she gave me a tour of on my visit. It was the beginning of a friendship.

After Sarah left I went to see my assistants. I sat in their office, wearing my evening gown and my 6-inch heels. I had not eaten a thing since the previous day and I so was exhausted I could hardly move.

My team told me that the young man I had danced with was part of the show – his name was Brahim Zaibat. He was Madonna's ex-boyfriend and the video of us dancing together was starting to create a buzz on the internet! I had not known who he was. He later admitted that he did not know who I was either. We were even.

My phone rang – it was François: 'Do you want to come and greet Merkel?'

He never normally suggested anything like that.

'When?'

'In five minutes.'

I could not meet her in an evening dress. I kicked off my shoes and took the stairs four by four to our private apartment. I hurriedly changed my dress and shoes and ran straight back down to wait in the hall by the President's side – ready to welcome the Chancellor.

Our exchange was pleasant. I was meeting her for the first time. She said she was pleased to meet me and would very much like it if we double-dated for the Bayreuth festival. I replied in the affirmative, saying I would be delighted. Then François and Angela Merkel went off for a working session before dinner.

I was finally able to go and rest before heading off to a long-standing dinner engagement I had.

I lay down on my bed, completely worn out. François' kindness that day had not been enough to make me forget the violence of his words the day before. When I got back from my dinner he was already asleep and he left for a European Council in Brussels the next morning. We barely had time to exchange a few words over breakfast. Discussing personal matters was not an option, as my son and the staff were there.

I decided to write him a long letter to take to Brussels and had it sent to his office. I explained that his behaviour the previous day was unacceptable: under French law he had a 'duty to assist', and he had failed even that by leaving me alone without calling a doctor. Had I still needed proof that he had fallen out of love with me, he had just given me undeniable evidence.

In my letter I told him I still loved him but that things could not go on as they were. Obviously I could understand his heavy workload and how difficult his role was to carry. But was it necessary, I asked, to be spiteful or – worse still – indifferent? Our love deserved more than that. How could power have stifled a love so strong, so violent? I felt stifled too. I needed to get some air. I needed him to show me some emotion and respect.

When he returned two days later we had a conversation. A difficult conversation. Incredibly so. He brought up the bad blood between us. He criticised me, said I had become impossible to live with. Unsurprisingly, since I was perpetually tense and nervous, animosity had grown between us – we had started clashing over nothing at all. His indifference affected me so much that I was in a state of permanent suffering.

I wasn't sure which one of us had changed.

He had started avoiding me, could no longer stand having me by his side in public. He did not consider me, he never looked at me or waited for me and his little asides to me were ever rarer. Even the photographers had noticed. Zoom lenses are to feelings what microscopes are to germs.

François reminded me of the 'tweet business': 'It caused

a lot of damage between us. Maybe we should have separated back then,' he said.

It struck me as unfair because he knew what was what. He was well aware of the circumstances. I am not trying to exonerate myself from this faux pas. I have borne all the consequences, and the incident continues to haunt me today, so I am fully aware that I was wrong. Yet, had he not lied to me that day – one time too many – nothing would have happened. I would not have written those few irreparable words.

The whole business started even before the presidential elections, when victory was in sight and Ségolène Royal was dreaming out loud of a prestigious post. After losing the presidential race five years earlier, her heart was set on becoming President of the National Assembly.

François and I had discussed it several times. He was not in favour of it.

He knew the price he would to have to pay if she succeeded – the political complications would be endless and the media would be merciless. No one could deny their personal links – and I would certainly never have presumed to do so. They have four children together – nothing is more precious. But Ségolène Royal's hypothetical ascension to the Presidency of the National Assembly would have fed the love triangle media machine – and we had all already suffered more than enough at its hands.

Several legal experts had also warned François that there was no precedent for a personal link between the executive power and the legislative power. And for good reason: the Constitution requires the separation of powers. Since 1875, the President is not allowed in the National Assembly or the Parliament.

Picture François Hollande as President and the mother of his children as President of the National Assembly. A sure-fire recipe for never-ending controversy. François knew it but he let Ségolène Royal chase after her dream regardless. In fact, he even encouraged her. He promised a prominent post when she rallied after the first round of the Socialist Party primary elections. Meanwhile she officially endorsed him, rather than backing his rival candidate, Martine Aubry. But, unofficially, he was adamant that he did not want her to be part of the State trinity. Such duplicitous behaviour did not surprise me. Countless times when he was First Secretary of the Socialist Party, I heard him encourage a candidate and then do everything in his power to prevent said candidate from getting the investiture.

He thought nothing of underhandedly blocking an election and letting other people carry the can. He was a politician through and through – it was written into every fibre of his body. Tactics were second nature to him.

After the first round of the June 2012 legislative

elections, Ségolène Royal was not in good stead. She had been parachuted to La Rochelle after leaving her historical fiefdom to another candidate. But the citizens of that city were attached to the local candidate, who had suddenly become, in the Socialist Party's official rhetoric, a party 'dissident'. Olivier Falorni was a long-term Socialist Party member and followed close on her heels in the first round of the elections.

I was at the electoral event held at the Élysée, in the green living room, which adjoins the presidential office. A couple of dozen computers had been set up on the table. There were a lot of people breaking down and analysing the results as they came in. I knew very few of them. Electoral fever had spread, the air was heavy with it – I knew and loved that atmosphere. A buffet was being served in the next room.

François analysed the results. The subtext was the Ségolène Royal issue. Shaking his head, he said: 'She doesn't stand a chance anymore. She is leading with 32 per cent, but Falorni is right behind with a 3 per cent gap. He is well established. He will easily gather support in the second round.'

'You won't do anything to support her, will you?' I asked.

'No,' he promised, 'you have nothing to worry about, I won't do anything, I have made a commitment not to.'

'Falorni is a good guy, he's always been loyal to you, you know that.'

'Yes, he's a good guy.'

Ever the conscientious politician, he nevertheless called the dissident candidate to – half-heartedly – ask him to stand down. Falorni refused to pull out of the race, and everyone was pretty clear on how things stood.

I went to bed a little before midnight. I was reassured, as I had feared more media frenzy. The press had had so much fun with our rivalry – the whole 'Hollande and his two women' ... It wounded me deeply. A few days before the 15 May 2012 inaugural ceremony, two journalists – journalists I knew well, at that – called me to ask whether I would be attending the ceremony.

One of them commented: 'Why would you be there if Ségolène Royal isn't?'

The other one asked: 'In what capacity will you be attending?'

My voice was trembling when I replied: 'I don't know. I am supposed to become First Lady, aren't I?' I felt so undermined that it was the best I could come up with.

I was unworthy in their eyes too. Even though I had been with François for five years – officially; in reality it was seven – I still had not earned my place by his side.

François had reassured me; I felt relieved that the spectre of an unmanageable ménage à trois was receding. We stayed at the Élysée apartment that night, rather than going home to rue Cauchy. I even slept on his side of the bed – I trusted him with every fibre of my being. He had a short night – he stayed up waiting for the full results. I did not hear him slide into bed next to me.

He left very early the next morning. We listened to the radio together, briefly – that was all we had time for. I took my time getting ready and went down to my office a little later. As usual, I went through the AFP feed on my iPhone. I suddenly discovered a news item marked 'Urgent': 'François Hollande supports Ségolène Royal.'

The news report stabbed me in the heart. The piece was understated: 'Ségolène Royal is the presidential majority's sole candidate in the Charente-Maritime constituency. She has my support and backing' – François Hollande, President, Monday 11 June 2012.

Which meant he had lied to me and, at the same time, reneged on a commitment he had made. Why had he not been honest the previous evening when he and I talked it over? Why had he not tried to explain that he had no other choice? Why not tell me that Ségolène Royal was putting pressure on him and that their children had interceded on their mother's behalf? I expect I would have raged against him at first but I would have bowed down eventually. He knows all too well that I am, first and foremost, a mother – I would have understood. He did not have the courage to come to me about it. He had just broken a public pledge he had brandished like an oath. To make matters worse, he had done it for personal reasons. And lied to me in the process. Again.

I called François immediately. I was fuming. I warned him I would support Falorni. I was outraged by the fate he had been abandoned to. After tirelessly devoting himself to his constituents for years, the Socialist Party had simply declared him a dissident candidate. It was a double sentence. François knew that he had pushed things too far this time, he knew that I was beyond furious. 'Hold on a minute! I'm on my way,' he said. 'Meet me upstairs.' Like an arsonist rushing to put out his own fire.

We met between the presidential floor and our room – in a room where Mitterrand had stored his books and his golf clubs. The Sarkozys had turned it into a children's room. I turned it into my office. I hung pictures of my sons when they were little and a few of my mementoes – mementoes I wanted to keep from the prying eyes of the visitors I saw in the formal office immediately below. I would always end up retiring to my office at some point in the day to escape the heavy atmosphere in the Palace.

But this time the tension had crept into the office. The atmosphere was oppressive, the way it is minutes before a storm, when the first dry flashes of lightning streak the sky and the crashes of thunder are coming. I was bursting with anger. It was our biggest fight since we had met. I could not fathom his betrayal. The very least he could have done was not to lie to me. If only he had been able to tell me face to face: 'Please understand, I have no choice – I have to do it for my children' … I can understand a mother's importance. I am a mother. I would have tried – I really would have tried – to recognise that. He did his best to calm me down, claiming he had had nothing to do with it and that the Secretary General of the Élysée had handled the whole thing. That was the *coup de grâce*: it was a ludicrous lie. The Secretary General himself later denied this pathetic fabrication. In fact, he had tried to stop Hollande from giving Ségolène Royal his support because it mixed everything up, personal life and public life. He was not the only adviser who tried to dissuade Hollande from backing her, either.

François did it anyway. His decision awoke my deep-rooted feeling of being illegitimate – a feeling that had deeply damaged me ever since we had made our relationship official. During our argument I warned François that I intended to tweet my support for Falorni. He did everything he could to stop me – even attempting to snatch my phone out of my hands – but gave up before things escalated any further. I sat on the small bed against the wall and started to write my 140 characters.

I deliberately chose to wish Olivier Falorni 'good luck',

rather than 'support' him. I thought that he might throw the towel in as a result of the President pledging his support to Ségolène Royal. I knew Falorni, in fact I had had a brief conversation on the phone with him the previous day. He was worried that the President might lend his rival a helping hand but I had reassured him that no such thing would happen. The President had personally guaranteed it. For all I knew, Falorni would be discouraged by the Socialist Party's betrayal and would stand down. I worded my tweet specifically so it would fit either scenario.

Anger clouded rationality. I wrote the message with a steady hand. My hand did not tremble either when I sent out the message to my Twitter followers. It was 11.56. 'Good luck to Olivier Falorni who has proved his worth and fought alongside the people of La Rochelle for many years with selfless commitment.'

I could not have imagined for a second the explosive reaction it would provoke. That short sentence spread like wildfire over the internet, it was picked up, retweeted, commented on millions of times and I was not aware of it. Blindsided by the President's lie, I walked right into the lion's den.

I immediately sent a text message to two people to inform them – Olivier Falorni and my Chief of Staff, Patrice Biancone. Patrice came to see me immediately.

He, for one, had realistically assessed the scale of the catastrophe. His phone started to vibrate non-stop, then mine followed suit. The press was out in force. I only answered the AFP's question: had my account been pirated or was I the person who had written that tweet? I owned my tweet. Then I retired, I locked myself up, cut myself off from the world – as I always do when my world is shaken.

In spite of everything I did not cancel my lunch with an editor. It had been arranged for my book review column in *Paris-Match*. Unsurprisingly, the first thing she mentioned was the tweet. Seeing that I had not realised how far-reaching the consequences of my actions had been, she told me what she had heard in the cab on her way – the growing controversy and bewilderment. It had made front covers all over the media, I had become the disgraced First Lady. The one who dared speak out about politics, the one who spoke out of line – opposing the President's official message. I was the destroyer of the Socialist Party's project and, above all, the jealous woman who wanted to see Ségolène Royal fall from grace.

Which is precisely the reason why the editor offered me an inordinate advance for a book contract. Naturally I turned it down on the spot.

François came to see me a few hours later. He too had immediately assessed the damage but he has a wonderful quality – he always looks forward and never dwells on what is done. How could we get out of this situation? That was the only thing he was concerned about. I had no idea. He was absolutely furious. He told me he planned to stay at the Élysée that evening and have dinner with his children and expected me to return home, to rue Cauchy, alone with my son. I did not argue.

The next day he met me at our flat but he was still angry and he barely said a word to me. He had built a wall of silence around himself – his silences always hurt me deeply. I hated those evenings when we were strangers to each other – alone together. I did not know whether he was even aware of it.

Since the next day was the second round of the legislative elections, François and his advisers were worried that the tweet would have a negative impact on the results. Comments from journalists and 'leading experts' in political forecasts amounted to the same thing: with these 140 characters I had just cost the Socialist Party at least fifty seats.

In spite of his irritation with me, François honoured a promise made to my youngest son. The three of us were meant to have dinner in a restaurant that François had wanted to take us to. François could have cancelled: I would have understood and so would Léonard. But over the last seven years François had seen my son grow. He had known him as a child and the two of them got on well. He wanted to make him happy and he kept his promise. Luckily, Léonard chatted away happily but on several occasions I caught François looking slightly lost. I realised how much I had hurt him.

I told him I was prepared to issue a public apology. He refused: he did not want me to make any more public statements. He was concerned it would only stoke up the fire. But the embers were still glowing and were not dying down; it was all still smouldering under the surface. I should have followed my instinct and released an apology statement.

I sent a text message to two of François' children to apologise. Thomas, his eldest, answered with harsh words. Implicitly, though, his message highlighted the heart of the matter: that he and his brothers and sisters – just like most children whose parents have started over with someone else – refused to accept his parents' separation. We were definitely caught up in a private imbroglio.

The next day, François and I went to a painting exhibition, right next to the Élysée. Obviously, you would have been hard pushed to say there was any warmth between us, François was very distant. In fact I saw him very little until the following Monday: he spent his time at the Élysée.

When we were alone, he would bring up my 'negative image'. He was worried I would become contagious. All he could think about was himself.

'What about me? Do you remember what your image was like when I fell in love with you? Had I not looked any further than your popularity I would not have loved you.' In 2005–06, François fared so badly in the polls that research institutes did not even count him.

So it was that on the night of the La Rochelle vote I was excluded from the electoral event. I did not so much as raise an eyebrow. I stayed alone in our flat on rue Cauchy. We messaged each other over the afternoon when the first trends started coming in. I could sense he was relaxing somewhat. The results were even better than the pre-tweet forecasts. My foul had not had the slightest impact on the Socialist Party's score. Ségolène Royal was not elected, but her low score in the first round was irredeemable.

Just like in the presidential elections in 2007.

Despite the fact that the presidential majority had scored very well overall, I did not receive much support in the days that followed. The Socialist Party's victory was expected, so my tweet was the more exciting event for the press – and they charged.

They painted Ségolène Royal as the victim of a blow below the belt rather than a candidate who had been unwisely parachuted into a constituency. In the eyes of the media and public opinion I was guilty of tripping her up. Guilty of intervening in a political debate to settle a private dispute. Guilty of not being in agreement with the President whose life I shared. Guilty of irrational jealousy. I was a woman who steals husbands, a homewrecker, spiteful and quick-tempered, hysterical. So many compliments … they were making me blush! Once again I offered to issue a public apology. Once again François' answer was a firm no.

I tried to escape the trial by mob. I shut everything out. I isolated myself. I would receive messages saying, 'Whatever you do, do not read this piece.' Which was like a taunt. Either I resisted and imagined the worse, or I read the piece and invariably it knocked the breath out of me. I had to endure calls to order from all the high-level state personalities and big names in the Socialist Party. They outdid each other to find the harshest things to say about me: the Prime Minister, the favourite candidate for National Assembly Presidency, the First Secretary of the Socialist Party, and even a long-term close friend of François … I could go on.

I know the political game. I spent fifteen years working as a journalist in that field. I knew none of them would have dared attack me without François' approval. One of my friends later phrased it in a horribly accurate way: 'It was Hollande himself who issued the licence to kill.'

I don't think I had ever felt so lonely. His anger at me fell after the second round of the elections – the Socialist

Party had done well – but he remained very harsh. I could not understand why the political leaders were not trying to play the whole thing down and move on to something else. Every day, one of them fuelled the controversy.

TO FIGHT OFF despair I escaped as often as I could to the park of Versailles and cycled until my muscles ached. During those moments I was less than certain that I would ever set foot in the Élysée again. The thoughts in my head were dark, very dark indeed. But I had to keep it together: two of my sons were about to sit their baccalaureate exam. An exam that came around when – symbolically – there was a price on their mother's head. And that very head was plastered on the back of all the news kiosks, crowned with titles that vied with each other to assassinate my character. What crime had I committed exactly? I was under fire for having a private life and a public life. That much was true. But I had not been the one to start it. François Hollande had only supported one candidate in the legislative elections and she happened to be the mother of his children. He had extended his support to no other candidate. He was the one who brought his personal life into the political sphere.

But my tweet had tainted the supreme symbol: the

mother, the blameless one. I too am a mother, but not to the President's children. It counted for nothing. A few months later a poll expert recommended bringing my children into public eye. He explained that French citizens never saw me with them and that a few well-placed and well-planned family pictures would be enough to turn public opinion around. Instead of seeing me as a 'mistress' they would see me as a mother and stepmother. He urged me to use my children to my benefit.

As for my image in the government, there were a few women in the Cabinet who did defend me. I was touched. One of them even explained that I had become a symbol in the *banlieues*. Young girls saw me as the woman who rejected the 'duty to obey'. To my surprise, when I was finally ready to face going out in the street I was greeted with words of sympathy and support – many of which were from young girls or women who came from immigrant backgrounds.

I had a lunch scheduled with the Minister for Women's Rights two or three days after the 'scandal'. I was convinced she would cancel on account of her close relationship with Ségolène Royal. She did no such thing. I was grateful for that. Obviously we soon got to the issue of the tweet. I expressed regret. But that was not what interested her: 'I am impressed by your media potency and I thought we could do some work together.'

I was stunned. Though I would have happily done without this 'media potency' – all those magazine covers that treated me like a mean and jealous witch – I thought it was brave on her part to want to be seen with me.

'What have you got in mind?' I asked.

'We could go talk to the prostitutes in the Bois de Boulogne together – at night.'

Her answer took me by surprise. I knew fighting prostitution was something she felt strongly about. But on that occasion I reacted with caution: 'I'm not sure it is a good idea under the current circumstances, I have to find issues people agree on.'

Though I turned down her offer, I remembered the expression she had used – the 'media potency' that so fascinated her. She was attracted by what I had been trying to avoid – and simply could not shake – since the start of my relationship with François Hollande.

I had become incapable of going to my office, I stopped going to the Élysée altogether. I carefully avoided Élysée advisers, whose hostility was tangible. Three of them, however, came to see me in secret to say they understood me and that the President had made a mistake releasing his statement of support. They even said they thought I had been his lightning rod. Had I not tweeted, the press's thunder would have fallen onto his head for supporting his former partner in an obvious mixture of worlds that should remain separate. A few editorials said as much, but they were few and far between.

It was June 2012. The doctors suggested that sedatives might help weather the violence of the attacks directed against my person. I said no. I had never taken anti-depressants and did not want to start. No doubt I overestimated my strength. With the benefit of hindsight I think this should have been the signal that forced me to realise I needed to take a break. That I needed to take care of myself and try to understand the infernal spiral we were caught up in and figure out how to loosen the noose. But I stayed alone with my thoughts.

While I was clocking up the kilometres on my bicycle at the weekend at La Lanterne, I reflected on what had pushed me to make this 140-character mistake. To begin with, my loyalty to Olivier Falorni, the double injustice he had suffered, but above all the impossible political situation that would have resulted from Ségolène Royal being elected. Him – President Hollande – at the Élysée Palace, and her at the helm of the National Assembly. A palace each. A split family reunited by power – one of them head of the Assembly that votes in the laws; and the other one implementing them. I could not see where I fitted into that picture. As things stood, finding my place was difficult enough! I had dropped a bomb and it had exploded in my face. No one does that without a reason. Simple lack of judgement cannot explain away everything.

The image I had been dragging behind me since the beginning of our relationship was not one I recognised. I was the person who split up 'the mythical couple in French politics'. The fact that when my relationship with François Hollande suddenly turned into love – nine years ago already! – I was also in a relationship was all too readily forgotten. It did not matter to anyone that I too had a family then: I had a husband I loved, Denis, and three young children.

We had all the ingredients for happiness, a lovely family life, a large house in the outskirts of Paris, a wonderful dog – who has just died, as I am writing these pages. The newspaper had agreed to let me have Wednesdays off to spend more time with my boys. I had gone from being someone who had defined herself by refusing to live the same life as my mother to wanting to be more like her.

I would make *crêpes* or waffles on Wednesday afternoons. We would go on walks – my children were still at the glorious age of building huts in the woods. I loved hanging around garden centres looking for new flowers to plant. I loved mowing the lawn and gardening. I eagerly awaited the spring, and lilacs, followed by the blossoming cherry trees. I loved all of that!

I resisted the attraction between François and me for

as long as I could. He was the one who was insistent, he was the one who suddenly switched our platonic friendly brand of love up a gear and turned it into passionate love.

Ultimately, I am the one who paid the price for that relationship. I had to leave political journalism. And in everyone's eyes I became the temptress, the nasty one, the homewrecker.

Starting over with a man who has a past is never easy. Millions of other women navigate the intricacies of blended families but Ségolène Royal's presence in the political arena made things even more complicated for François and me.

I can also appreciate just how difficult it was for her. Consecutive presidential elections – in 2007 and five years later, in 2012 – saw over sixteen million French citizens twice cast their vote for the Socialist Party. Only, the first time, the ballot paper had her name on it and five years later, it bore his. An unusual, if not unique, situation. At least, until now. If Hillary Clinton runs, she will find herself in a comparable situation.

I remember discussing Hillary's candidacy with François during a walk in the gardens of the Élysée Palace. 'It would be grotesque for her to run for President after her husband,' he said.

I was taken aback: 'Have you forgotten that you ran for President after Ségolène Royal, and that you were even up against each other during the Socialist Party primaries?' In François Hollande's mind, the two of them are above the rules he holds others to. He lives his life in constant denial.

In the French collective consciousness – and, no doubt, in my mind as well – the two of them are the de facto couple. The mother of his children is his 'official' partner. I was always the other woman. And yet I have never loved anyone the way I loved him.

I have made many sacrifices for him, unreciprocated. He did refer to me on one occasion as the love of his life when speaking to the press. 'Succeeding in your personal life and meeting the love of your life is exceptional good fortune. This sort of fortune can pass. I seized it. I have been sharing my life with Valérie Trierweiler for several years now, to my great joy.' He later publicly expressed regret at having used the phrase 'love of his life' – to spare his children's feelings, and perhaps to smooth over popular opinion. What a disappointment … What was I to him?

I felt that I had no legitimacy – something we often discussed. He did not see the problem, since we lived together and loved each other. One day, I plastered our kitchen wall with photos of my ex-husband and me from back when we were married: snaps of happy moments and holiday embraces. He was shaken. That day, he understood how difficult it was for me to live with the relentless media coverage of his former life with Ségolène Royal. He understood that I needed his support and recognition. Alas, it was short-lived. On the day of the explosive tweet, years of suffering came to a head. I was the one to trigger the detonator, and for that I take full responsibility. But it was François Hollande and Ségolène Royal, with their never-ending games – mixing private and public spheres, using family pictures and ambiguous statements – who built the ticking bomb.

One minute they were going head to head, the next they were using each other as stepping stones. In 1997, when the Plural Left won the legislative elections – called early following the dissolution of the National Assembly – François besieged the Prime Minister with appeals to appoint Ségolène Royal in the new Cabinet. Meanwhile, François took the helm of the Socialist Party. Ségolène Royal had to be kept busy so he could do as he pleased. The Prime Minister eventually submitted to his wishes.

Seventeen years later, Ségolène Royal reappeared in the current government because François Hollande had willed it so. The political play between them is endless; it is a maze I got lost in.

In March 2014, two months after our separation, I went to vote in the municipal elections. Near Isle-Adam, 40 km outside of Paris, where I used to live with my family – the family I had built before I met François. My heart sank as I parked my car in front of our old house, which my ex-husband still lives in.

I walked past my children's primary school. A small, old-fashioned school with only seventy pupils, split into three classes. The school sits on the village square, opposite a twelfth-century church. All three of my children attended it. Memories came flooding back, overwhelming me. I remembered my three beautiful boys, in the morning, at panic time. We lived so close to the school that we could hear the bell ring. That was the signal to start the hunt for a pair of shoes, a coat or a school book. And demand a goodbye kiss. Afterwards, I would go for a walk in the countryside with my ex-husband and our dog.

I was overcome by a wave of nostalgia. My children were nearly grown men. Our polling station was in 'The Dreaming House', their old canteen. When I walked out that day, I cared little about the Socialist Party's results – what mattered to me was what I had done with my life. I had just voted Socialist, but I was thinking about my family – the brilliant man I had married and my wonderful boys, whom I had left for François seven years earlier. Nobody believed in him then, and I was far from nursing secret dreams of the Élysée. We had never discussed the possibility of him running for President one day. There was nothing but love.

All those sacrifices only to be thrown out like a used

handkerchief – in the blink of an eye, and in eighteen words. Did I make the right choice? Crippled with doubt, I decided to go for a walk in the countryside to think things over, the way I used to do. Heavy hail forced me to turn back hastily. To turn back – at that moment I longed to turn back time, for those years never to have happened...

But how could I forget those first few years of passion with François? That once-in-a-lifetime passion that devours everything. How could I not reminisce about the time 'Before Us', as we used to say? All those years when I covered the Socialist Party as a political journalist. First, in a publication called *Profession Politique*[5] – where I started out, along with a dozen other young journalists.

I had never dreamt of being a journalist: it seemed completely inaccessible. Which is why I felt like I had found my own Holy Grail when the opportunity arose – thanks to an extraordinary series of fortunate events – twenty-six years ago.

The year of my Masters of Advanced Studies in Political and Social Sciences and Communication at the Sorbonne, I was among guests at a party held for the 1988 presidential election. Shuffling between different groups of people,

---

5  *Profession: Politician.*

I was dragged along to the Maison de l'Amérique Latine, where François Mitterrand was celebrating his victory. When he saw me at the venue, he greeted me and said: 'I believe we have met.'

No, of course not. I did not know the President! I was twenty-three years old, a small-town girl who had landed in Paris five years earlier to study and follow her first love. I did not know anyone 'important' – least of all the President…

But that short exchange caught the attention of an investor in the publication *Profession Politique*, which was due to launch three months later. 'Go and see them,' he said, 'they are looking for young people.'

It was May, and I was about to finish my studies the following month. I had a few job leads in public relations, which I was chasing half-heartedly. I was struggling with the notion that my studies were coming to an end – I enjoyed student life. Still, I contacted the head of *Profession Politique*, with no belief in my chances of being recruited.

I was convinced I did not have the right profile. I was not a female Rasputin. Like many others, I was full of self-doubt, having been stalled by that infamous glass ceiling. But this time, I felt carried by new-found strength. I went for one interview, then a second. And – nothing short of a miracle – I was offered the position. I was due to start work at *Profession Politique* on 1 August.

There was one problem. Like every year for the past five years, I had committed to working all summer at Byblos, a shop selling ethnic jewellery in Saint-Gilles-Croix-de-Vie, a seaside resort in Vendée – the region where I spent all of my childhood holidays with my parents and my brothers and sisters. First, in a small rental house back when we went on holiday in June because prices were affordable – which also meant that we missed a month of school. Then, when we got a little older, camping became the family's seasonal migration. My parents had finally been able to buy a second-hand caravan but we lacked basic amenities, since we did not stay at a camping site but in a field which a farmer rented out to two or three families.

To pay for my studies, I complemented the state grants I received with other odd jobs and summer seasonal work in the shop. From the age of eighteen, I had single-handedly supported myself. My parents had let me leave home on the condition that I managed on my own. They could not afford to do otherwise. They were not in a position to help me financially and it would not have occurred to me to ask them for anything. I still remember my mother crying when I 'moved to the capital'…

That is why, five years later, I had to call the shop owners to tell them that I would be starting full-time employment on 1 August, but that I was prepared to work for them throughout July. They agreed – they were happy for me, and proud of me. Over the years, they have become real friends – more than that, in fact: they are family to me. I owe them a lot. I never lost touch with them. They came to see me at the Élysée Palace, intimidated to see me there, thirty years after working as a sales assistant in their shop.

When August came around, I became increasingly anxious. Would I be up to the task of being a journalist? No, I would never be good enough. I was interested in politics, but I was no expert.

We did not yet have a full team. The office was empty. We assembled the IKEA desks ourselves. I needed to improve my IT skills – I had never owned a computer. I learned fast. We were able to start work on a 'zero issue'. Then came the first issue, the launch issue. I was lucky enough to get a scoop. Secret plans to hold grouped elections, which the then Minister of the Interior was concocting. The topic made the cover of the first issue. The editor-in-chief congratulated me. 'I was just lucky,' I said. I will never forget his answer: 'A good journalist is a lucky journalist, nothing more, nothing less.' Nor will I forget what he said next – that lesson is indelibly imprinted on my mind: 'Remember that you only exist through your newspaper, not through yourself.'

That is how I came to cover the Élysée, part of the government, and the Socialist Party, no less! I was asked for a paper on the 'resurgence of old factions in the Social-ist Party'. I looked up from my work and asked naively: 'What are factions?'

The editor-in-chief looked at me in despair and answered: 'If it had been up to me, you would never have been hired.'

I was well aware of my shortcomings. I had not attended Sciences Politiques Paris; there was so much I did not know. I lacked political culture – culture full stop, for that matter. I did not know the protocol in this new world.

I was twenty-three and had never boarded a plane. When I said as much to the civil aviation director, whom I had been assigned to write a profile of, he offered to organise my maiden flight! The only foreign country I had been to was Germany, on a language exchange. I had never seen the Mediterranean. As a child, I had only been to the theatre once, and it was a musical at that. A cinema outing was a rare occurrence. The Parisian scene was foreign to me. When the director of the paper told me that to do well you had to 'dine out in town', I did not understand what he was talking about. 'In town', for the provincial girl that I was, meant taking the bus to go into town. And not for dinner either – we never went to the restaurant.

But I got down to work. I tried to study and understand

the factions and sub-factions of the Socialist Party: those loyal to Chevènement, Mauroy, Poperen, Fabius, Jospin and the 'Transcourants' – a transfactional faction.[6] One of the leaders of the latter movement was called Fran-çois Hollande. He and his friends were close to Jacques Delors, they were open-minded and iconoclastic. I felt a political affinity with the group.

I still own a few copies of their periodical, *Témoin*.[7] On my bookshelf, I also have François Hollande's first book, *L'heure des choix*,[8] which he co-wrote with Pierre Moscovici and published in 1991. His autograph reads: 'To Valérie Massonneau [my maiden name] who after reading this book will grow from a formidable expert on the mysteries of politics, into an authority on economics.'

François Hollande and I have known each other since 1988. He has been in my world for twenty-six years. I have no memory of our first lunch. He remembers it, however, and has often complained since that I have forgotten that moment. It was at the restaurant of the National Assembly, I know that much.

I remember the Transcourants meetings of Lorient in Brittany with more clarity. Every summer, Jacques

---

6   A reformist faction of the Socialist Party.

7   *Witness.*

8   *The Hour of Choice.*

Delors chaired these focus days. There were rainy years –
Brittany is what it is – but the meetings were always cheerful regardless. François brought the good mood – as he
does everywhere he goes. Not many journalists attended.
We went out for a drink at the end of the day. I enjoyed
being around him. François liked journalists and before
long I was his favourite.

In 1989, *Profession Politique* changed hands and a new
editor-in-chief was appointed.

He took an instant disliking to me, and I was quickly
off the team. He mistook me for a *bourgeoise*, from a
well-to-do family.

Since I had been laid off and had cashed in a redun-
dancy package, I decided to spend a month in the US
with Frank, my first love – who was to become my first
husband. It was time for me to start discovering the world
and I had a few job options lined up. A few months earlier I had met the editor-in-chief of *Paris-Match* at the
Élysée during the traditional media conference where
the President addresses the nation to present his New
Year Wishes. That day, a more experienced colleague had
said: 'Stay with me – after the ceremony Mitterrand will
be seeing a dozen journalists in one of the living rooms.
I'll bring you along.'

And so I found myself devotedly listening – along
with the elite of the press – to the then President. The

*Paris-Match* editor-in-chief saw me leave the living room with that privileged group of journalists and we exchanged details. I was only twenty-four and François Mitterrand had impacted my fate for the second time! How could I have imagined that one day I would be with another President? That I too would tread the red carpet rolled out in the Élysée Palace's *Cour d'honneur* for the inauguration ceremony? When it did happen I tried to find the living room in question. I remembered that it was next to the function room but I could not recognise it with complete certainty. Twenty-five years had elapsed. Twenty-five years! The years had gone by in a flash. I had been married twice and had divorced twice.

I had given birth to my three boys: they were by far my main concern and my most wonderful success – they were the people I held dearest in the world.

I walked into *Paris-Match* on tiptoes in 1989. I started out as a freelance journalist; I was not yet part of the editorial team. A young 'on-the-field' reporter was needed for the new political pages of *Paris-Match*. Since I had a few left-minded contacts I was quite naturally oriented towards the Socialist Party. I also had a few passes to the Élysée – which was uncommon for a young journalist. *Paris-Match* veterans in charge of politics were hardly delighted that I had been recruited. Six months later, the newspaper's legendary boss, Roger Thérond, hired me at the bottom of the pecking order as a contributor. That was all it took to spark envy and feed all sorts of fantasies, with improbable lists of whom I owed my recruitment to. I discovered corridor gossip very early on!

I did not meet Roger Thérond when I was hired. I met him few months later in rather unpleasant circumstances. I was what was called a 'regular contributor' and did not have an official contract. I would submit articles that would appear – or not – in the paper. One of my articles did not sit well with the infamous businessman Bernard Tapie.

I had been invited by 'Club Mendès France' – a group of young people fresh out of the elite École nationale d'administration – to one of their debate dinners … guest-starring Bernard Tapie. I arrived five minutes late and found that they had already sat down to dinner. The then head of Marseilles football club welcomed me with this sentence: 'Don't tell me she went to the École nationale d'administration – you can tell just by looking at her.' I did my best to keep a low profile. At the time I was still shy. I was introduced to Bernard Tapie as a journalist, which was further evidenced by the fact that I always had my little notebook handy. But Mr Tapie wasn't one to be easily put off: 'No problem! With me, nothing is off the record, I take responsibility for everything I say.'

Mr Tapie, politician that he was, blamed François Mitterrand for the rise of the National Front. He went on to list the various people he despised, and finally attacked government ministers: none of them were as well off as he was, his mansion was bigger than their ministry, and so on and so forth. It was a full-on Tapie fest, replete with Tapie-phrases and bragging. I pitched a piece to *Paris-Match*, which was immediately accepted.

When it came out, Bernard Tapie called Roger Thérond and certified that … I had made everything up. The editor-in-chief called me in and asked me to confirm I had attended that dinner. I explained myself and showed her my notepad.

It was not enough and the whole business did not stop there: I was called in to 'see Roger'. Though I had never been called in to see the headmaster at school, I felt like I was a bad pupil who had been dealt her punishment. I did not feel confident. I made the École nationale d'administration graduates aware of Bernard Tapie's reaction: they had read my article and knew that what I had reported was accurate. Their outrage somewhat reassured me ahead of the meeting. I was nervous when I entered the 'boss's office'. He was not a man to be messed with and his enunciation was impeccable. I barely dared open my mouth.

'I was told I could trust you but I do not know you,' he said. 'If you could prove that Bernard Tapie said what you say he did, it would be easier.'

It was my first hurdle as a journalist. I was in luck once again. The debate had been recorded. The two organisers of the political debate club were prepared to support me and hand over the recording to Roger Thérond. They were seen a few days later. They brought the tape but the director of *Paris-Match* was satisfied just seeing the evidence without listening to it. What mattered was that I was being backed up, that I took my work seriously. Rather than take responsibility for what he had said, Bernard Tapie had tried to have me fired. Instead of that, his abortive tactic got me officially integrated at *Paris-Match*!

I remember later telling François Hollande – who already distrusted the businessman – this story. At the time, we bumped into one another every week in the famous Hall of the Four Columns at the National Assembly. He was one of the MPs who attracted journalists. He was skilled at extracting spice from political life. He had a journalist's thinking cap, and could make you change angles for your article without you even realising.

The years passed and we were getting closer, professionally speaking. Early 1993, I took a few months off for my first maternity leave. I had met at *Paris-Match* the man who was to become my husband two years later, Denis Trierweiler – an editor at the newspaper, as well as a translator and an expert on German philosophers. He was handsome and intelligent but had an inner darkness. He came from a background that was even more under-privileged than mine. He had that specialist knowledge I so sorely lacked. But he stayed locked up in his own world, his books, his philosophy and his thirst for knowledge. Even before we were in a relationship, I had dreamt he would be the father of my children. He had dreamt the same dream. Starting a family with him was the most natural thing in the world.

Our son was born in January and it was in the rue de Solférino – the Socialist Party HQ – that I resumed work for the event for the legislative elections on 21 March. That evening the Socialist Party suffered a flat-out defeat. The atmosphere was moribund. I wondered what I was doing there – why I had left my baby at home, my baby who was not yet three months old – for this tragic atmosphere.

Like most Socialist MPs, François Hollande was ousted by the right. He was in a state of shock. The two of us met for lunch shortly afterwards, at a restaurant called La Ferme Saint-Simon. He opened up to me, trusted me with his doubts and questions about his political future. He lived and breathed politics but had been shaken by this failure. He was wondering whether to give up Corrèze and choose another constituency. The problem was that it was tricky for the Socialist Party to maintain its influence in Corrèze as it was in the middle of a Chirac stronghold.

I was struck by Hollande's sincerity that day. Contrary

to his habit, he did not overdo high spirits and humour. I remember how lost he looked. Real exchanges, trusting exchanges, are few and far between in a political journalist's career. Notwithstanding, our relationship was anything but ambiguous. François Hollande never said a word out of line to me or behaved inappropriately with me – unlike many a politician.

There were only fifty-two Socialist MPs left – which was hardly enough to keep a journalist busy full-time. The *Paris-Match* board asked me to focus on covering Édouard Balladur's government. And so I met the right-wing leaders. My address book was filling up. François Hollande and I lost touch somewhat.

I found the time to have a second child. Those interludes that give the tempo of a mother's life are both precious and unique. My eldest son was born in the middle of the legislative elections; the second arrived in the middle of the 1994 European vote! For a political journalist, my timing could have been better but I did not care. I loved my job but the maternal instinct was stronger. Two years later, I was pregnant again.

I come from a big family, and the age gap between us is small – my parents had six children in four and a half years. That's right, four and a half years! Twins followed by a child every year. Not only that, but my mother gave birth to her sixth child five days after her twentieth birthday.

The black-and-white pictures of my mother – so young – with her brood around her and in her arms are an inspiration to me. She is beautiful and we could not have had a better mother. She is a role model for me: she has always managed; she was strong and never shied away from her responsibilities.

She did not have a car and every day she would climb onto her bike and go grocery shopping for nine people (my maternal grandmother lived with us). There were three of us on her bike when she took us to school. She also had to take care of my father, who was disabled and tyrannical. He had had a leg amputated in 1944, aged twelve, as a result of shrapnel. We had always known our father with his wooden leg. In our eyes, he wasn't disabled. He could not stand the word and wore the title of *Grand Invalide de Guerre*[9] with much more pride. I remember one of my friends who told me in primary school: 'If my father was like yours, I would cry every day.'

I was perplexed. I did not understand what I should have been crying about.

When my father died in 1986, he had never talked to us about his 'accident'. During François' presidential campaign, a journalist from the regional daily *Ouest-France* managed to dig up an article about that tragic day. A

---

9 Severely disabled war veteran.

driver had found three young boys on the roadside, one of them was dead and the other two were injured. My father was unconscious. They managed to save him, but not his leg. No doubt he also left his joie de vivre in that ditch. The day I read that article – it was just a brief, in fact – I understood what my father's personal tragedy had been. It was then that I cried, by myself, thinking about what he had gone through.

At school, when we filled in the 'profession' of our parents, we had to write 'GIG' (*Grand Invalide de Guerre*) next to 'father' and 'no profession' next to 'mother'. Our 'difference' lay right there. Our parents did not work. They stayed at home. Which meant that for us, hanging around after school was out of the question. We did not have much freedom. Time was never wasted: as soon as we got home we had our snack – jam or fake Nutella – and then we would settle around the table in a room we called the 'family room'. We did our homework there while my mother presided at the end of the table with her knitting – always prepared to help us recite the poems we had to learn by heart or practise our times tables.

My mother helped us as long as she could – she had only completed primary education. I admired her but I had sworn to myself that I would not live the same life as her. She was a slave to a large family and never had any time for herself – she didn't allow herself any. For most of her life, my mother had to put up with more than a person should ever have to put up with.

She had incredible inner strength and was driven to be independent. She learned to drive without telling our father; she had only let us in on the secret so we could cover for her. When she passed her licence not only did my father agree to let her drive him around, but my parents bought a family-size Peugeot 404 with three rows of seats. The children rode at the back with the very youngest sat in the middle. That was the beginning of Sunday drives. We visited a lot of castles – we got in for free thanks to our 'large family' card.

My mother had another major achievement, again without my father knowing: she looked for a job. It was 1982. I was already seventeen. She applied for a cashier position at the Angers skating rink and got the job. My father struggled with the idea of her getting her independence. It wasn't as if she hadn't already worked occasionally, though. She would give one of my uncles a hand with his flower stall at the market on some Saturdays. I adored meeting her there and helping her wrap up the bouquets. But this time it was a full-time job with set shifts – very late some evenings and every weekend.

Like many other women, her life became a race against the clock. Unlike most other women, she had six children and a disabled husband who was becoming increasingly dictatorial with age and illness. She would run in to cook a dinner which she did not have time to eat with us; eventually she would sit down for five minutes and gulp down a few mouthfuls, straight out of the Tupperware.

My three sisters and I helped her with cooking and housework. My father had excused my two brothers – the boys – from all housework save taking the bins out. The boys' studies were more important than the girls'. My mother encouraged me to break away from this pattern, to escape from this vision of a woman's role. In secondary school I started to work every Sunday morning in a shop called Tout et tout,[10] making 50 francs for four hours' work. And that was how I bought my freedom – otherwise known as a second-hand moped.

At sixteen I had temporary jobs after school. In my last year at school I worked as a receptionist at the Palais des Congrès.[11] Clad in my navy blue and white uniform, I would usher people who were fortunate enough to see the show to their seats. Whenever possible I would linger to see what I could.

I felt the sting of injustice early on when one of my school friends told me her parents did not want me to

---

10 Anything and Everything.

11 A convention centre.

come to her house anymore. I did not live on the right side of the boulevard, I did not belong to the right social circles, I was not a suitable person to be seen with. I was the top student but I did not have the right profile. The whole story really affected me – it has always stayed with me. I abhor racial discrimination but I think we often forget just how pernicious social discrimination can be.

I left Angers, my underprivileged *banlieue* and my family – on the very day the baccalaureate results were published. The next day, I enrolled for a history degree at Nanterre University. I was moving from a small town to Parisian life; from a school in a building listed as a national heritage site to a suburban university that was a hotbed for the May '68 uprisings; from life at home with my family to a bohemian couple life in a shoebox attic room. Two years later, my father died.

François Hollande heard my backstory early on. Even though I was the journalist who was supposed to get him to confide in me and share some political secrets, he was very good at making other people talk. He would some-times tease me good-humouredly by calling me Cinderella over those first few years when we only saw each other once in a while. I struck him as lacking self-confidence and all in all very different from my colleagues. Because I did not like to put myself forward I acquired a reputa-tion as a cold and haughty woman – a reputation which has stuck. At the National Assembly and at *Paris-Match* I was often portrayed as a *bourgeoise*. It amused me – me, the girl from Monplais', in a northern *banlieue* of Angers.

I was simply not like them, whatever they may have thought – the differences were blatantly obvious. I started dressing differently from other young people as soon as I could. I did not want to be the pauper, I wanted to be elegant and stand out. For years my youngest sisters and I only wore hand-me-downs from our older sisters. We had 'Sunday clothes' (itchy flannel trousers) which my grandmother had cut out of my father's trousers.

One of my worst memories is having to wear my brother's 'clodhoppers' to primary school. My shoes must have broken that day and my mother hadn't found an alternative solution. I refused to go to school wearing them. In the end, I wasn't given a choice and cried all the way to school. I sat in a corner during the break – not moving an inch, my feet hidden under my satchel.

Most of my colleagues waiting outside the Council of Ministers or in the Four Columns Hall at the National Assembly wore jeans. I wore skirt suits. Even at Nanterre University I wore skirts and retro jackets I bought at bargain prices at the Saint-Ouen flea market. My look merely reinforced my reputation as a hardened and disdainful young woman. Few of my colleagues dared approach me.

I gradually made friends with other journalists. Some

of my colleagues used me as 'bait' – in their own words. I became part of a group of only male journalists. We took politicians – male and female – out for lunch. We were new to the job so we joined forces. During one of those lunches I learned a very valuable lesson. A Cabinet reshuffle was taking place the following day and a centrist politician swore to us that he would never join Mitterrand's Cabinet. Three days later he was appointed a minister. I called him immediately and said, 'I wanted to thank you. Because of you I know that you should never believe a politician.' I should have remembered that…

In 1997 when Lionel Jospin was appointed Prime Minister, François Hollande became the Socialist Party's First Secretary. We had developed a strong bond and were growing closer. He made me laugh. His intelligence and sharp mind amazed me. He got from A to B so quickly! It didn't matter what the question was, he always had a quick answer that made perfect sense and was invariably witty. Our closeness amused some of my colleagues. They stayed close to me at the National Assembly, convinced that the First Secretary would make his remarks to me first. He did so without fail. And so my colleagues winked away merrily when he walked through the National Assembly towards our little group.

He would often call me on Mondays when *Paris-Match* wrapped on the grounds that I might need some piece of information or other – even though I had not tried to contact him. He also called me on Saturday afternoons when he was in Corrèze. He tipped me off but I also shared information with him because I knew the Socialist Party well.

As years went by our bond grew stronger. One election weekend I was covering him with a photographer in Corrèze. On Saturday evening he had dinner with us. Afterwards he had to attend a ball for elderly people. He decided to ride with us rather than with his driver. I drove because my photographer wanted to be able to get out as quickly as possible – as soon as there was a picture to take. 'Hollande' – that was what I called him then, I even still used the formal 'vous' – sat in the front with me. I was not much used to driving back then. My stiletto heels were too high and would be a nuisance for the clutch. So I took them off as soon as we got into the car and plonked them into his hands. François never forgot that.

Once we got to the ball he did his bit and danced with the little old ladies. I looked on, amused. He looked much less so. He was holding in his arms a lady who was in her eighties. I knew full well that it was not what he wanted at that particular moment.

The Jospin years (1997–2002) brought us closer together. We talked politics for hours on end. Before the summer holidays, late July, we had gotten into the habit of having lunch together so he could tell me about his plans for September.

In 2000, he took me out for lunch in the garden of the Maison de l'Amérique Latine. I was convinced that Jean-Pierre Chevènement would resign from his role as Minister of the Interior over a disagreement with Jospin about the Corsica issue. François Hollande, who was still the First Secretary of the Socialist Party, did not share my point of view. Barely a month later I was vindicated.

There we were, the two of us good-humouredly discussing this and that, when suddenly I saw Ségolène Royal heading straight for our table. When I told François – who had his back to the entrance of the restaurant – he thought I was joking. Until she sat down at our table. Her demeanour was ice-cold: 'Caught red-handed. I hope I'm not interrupting anything.'

François couldn't say a word. I was the one who answered, 'Not at all, we were talking about the Tour de France.'

'Stop taking me for a fool!'

'I'm perfectly serious. It's true. Besides, we weren't doing anything wrong. We are not in a hotel, are we?'

My aplomb irritated and impressed her in equal measures.

She turned to him and said: 'You never take *me* to places like this.'

It was a heated discussion. If one-sided: François didn't pipe a word. He was embarrassed by her making a scene. Eventually she got up and left as quickly as she had come – before things took a turn for the worse.

'It's not always easy for me, you know,' François said in a weak voice.

'Either way, you had better run after her,' I answered.

He thanked me and left. I stayed at the table alone, completely stunned by the whole ludicrous situation. Alone with a bill I would be paying off for a long time. Ségolène Royal's suspicion struck me as completely unjustified, let alone turning up unannounced at the restaurant. I now understand her. She had instinctively picked up on a danger I had not sensed myself.

The presidential campaign was drawing nearer. We continued to see each other in a strictly professional context. At least, I convinced myself that was the case.

He offered to help me write the narrative of the campaign – the deal was that we would meet regularly and he would share the hidden agenda of politics with me. I turned the offer down immediately. I sensed that I needed to maintain some distance between us. I enjoyed his company, he enjoyed mine. Our closeness was not quite normal and I felt that I needed to protect myself.

We saw each other rarely during Lionel Jospin's presidential campaign but we spoke on the phone frequently.

I followed Jospin closely, travelling across France on his campaign trail. I built strong friendships with some of my colleagues during that period, namely Patrice Biancone, who followed me to the Élysée. François Hollande envied us journalists for being involved in those moments. He envied us for being a part of the excitement surrounding the favourite in the presidential election. Meanwhile, he held his meetings separately and few journalists covered him. I bumped into him at Jospin's major regional meetings – the only ones he attended.

On 21 April 2002, Lionel Jospin lost the presidential race in the first round, with Jean-Marie Le Pen, the far-right leader, coming in second, after Jacques Chirac. It was a major upheaval. That evening, the campaign HQ, l'Atelier, was a picture of bleakness and dejection. I tried and failed to hide my tears. I was filled with the same despair and anger as everyone around me.

The crowd of despondent party members scattered. It was gone midnight. I went for a drink with a group of journalists. We discussed the title I had found for one of my articles about the defeated candidate: 'Élysée or Isle of Rhé for Jospin?' Unlike many of my colleagues, I was not surprised when Jospin announced he would retire from politics on the very evening of his defeat. François Hollande was gobsmacked by my clairvoyance. Hollande livened up the evening by making us all laugh. He chose to face a tragic situation with humour – as was his habit. Humour was his shield, his mask. Suddenly the laughter stopped: Ségolène Royal had just arrived. Hollande's persona changed immediately. He left with her. But he turned back for one last look at me. That one look left me inexplicably flustered.

That dark day, 21 April 2002, when the far-right party Front National outscored the Socialist Party was traumatising for my group of journalist friends – as it was of course for all of the members of the Socialist Party. Hollande was on the front line and granted me the first interview about the lessons to be learned from this catastrophe. We were alone in his office. He sat very close to me but I discreetly changed seats. Later, he would often remind me of how ill at ease I was with him.

We continued to talk very frequently. It was then that the first rumours of an affair between us started. I wasn't worried about it. Everyone knew my situation: my children and my husband, who also worked at *Paris-Match*. The closeness between François Hollande and me was anything but news – there had been no change there.

I was not yet aware of the electromagnetic field that sparked between the two of us as soon as we were together. From the outside it was obvious that something was going on. But I was blind, I could not see the love that was blossoming between us. Granted, there was a very real bond between us. Possibly even a friendship between a man and a woman that was tinged with seduction. But no more than that.

Some time later Ségolène Royal came to talk to me in the Hall of the Four Columns at the National Assembly: 'I would like to meet with you.'

'Of course, when?'

'Saturday.'

'No, not Saturday, I'll be with my children, I don't work on Saturdays.'

'Monday nine o'clock then.'

Her tone suffered no discussion.

When we met in her office at the National Assembly she greeted me frostily: 'You do know why I wanted to see you?'

I did not let her intimidate me. I had nothing to feel ashamed about.

'I think I could hazard a guess.'

'So you know about the rumour,' she said.

I did. But rumours had always circulated about everyone and everything and they always would – especially between male politicians and journalists. It was no reason to credit them.

She seemed surprised by my composure and the authority with which I spoke. She mellowed somewhat and asked me how to prevent this false information from spreading. I suggested a dinner as a foursome – my husband, François

Hollande and her – in a well-known restaurant, and she did not seem opposed to the idea. As for my husband, he knew about the whole business: I had always told him everything, I had nothing to hide from him.

The following day I left for a three-day trip to India covering Jean-Pierre Raffarin's official visit as France's new Prime Minister. When I got home, my husband told me that Ségolène Royal had called him and asked to meet. She had gone too far this time. I went straight to my office at *Paris-Match* to call her: 'What are you playing at? You're the one who is in the public eye, not me. You are the one who is taking risks by accrediting a rumour, not me. See him if you feel like it, you'll see he's a charming man.'

Until then, I had not really considered a romantic relationship with François Hollande. The intervention of a woman who feared our love above all else no doubt played a part in it becoming a possibility in my eyes. Not that I had consciously understood that yet – it was still a blur in my mind.

AT THE TIME of writing, Ségolène Royal has just been integrated in the Cabinet as Minister for the Environment. Blast from the past: as the news made a point of reminding us, she had already been given that portfolio twenty-two years earlier in Pierre Bérégovoy's government. The same year, she had given birth to her youngest daughter.

That year, 1992, I was also pregnant – with my first son. *Paris-Match* assigned me on an interview with her at the maternity ward. I knew that François Hollande and his press officer were against it. I told the magazine they shouldn't count on it – Ségolène Royal was sure to say no. I had barely got home from work when my landline rang. It was my editor-in-chief and he was beyond furious: 'For your information Ségolène Royal has just let TF1 cameras into her room at the maternity ward. You'd better secure an interview too.'

I couldn't believe it. I did as I was told and called the hospital switchboard. I was put straight through to Ségolène Royal and asked her if I could get some pictures. She agreed in exchange for an interview on the environment. The picture was taken without me being there and we did the interview by fax; I wrote the piece without us ever meeting. I certainly did not barge into her personal space to steal the father of her children – as was printed later, when our entire story was rewritten, twisted and endlessly reinterpreted. How could anyone imagine I would hatch such a Machiavellian plan when I was pregnant with my first child and had never been happier?

The following year I gave birth to my second child, and got married before the third one was born. I had no other plans than to build both my personal life and my career – François Hollande was not part of either of these plans. I even changed my surname. I wanted to be called Trierweiler. I wanted to show that I belonged to my husband. I will admit that the attacks hurt me because they touched on what was most precious to me.

While Ségolène Royal worried about rumours, the Socialist Party's debacle in 2002 sent me a little further to the right professionally speaking. I was often asked to cover President Chirac's trips. At first I sensed that the staff in the Élysée's press office was wary of me but gradually I gained their trust. Even though *Paris-Match*'s 'yellow pages' – the politics pages – were now considerably less interested in the Socialist Party, I did not abandon ship.

François Hollande and I had lunch once in a while – either alone or with other journalists. I had moved out of Paris with my family and he often 'saw me to the door over the phone': we would chat as I drove home even when it was very late. We never ran out of things to talk about.

With the 2004 regional elections fast approaching, politics were current affairs again.

Hollande had earned his stripes thanks to the Socialist Party's sweeping victory. The weekly newspaper *Le Point* made him 'man of the year'. Because Hollande was at the forefront of the regional campaign, I travelled hundreds of miles with him. For the first and only time, I wrote a positive article about him. I remember a comment the *Paris-Match* editor-in-chief made: 'So now you're tagging along behind Hollande.'

## 2014...

Late afternoon on rue Cauchy, spring is only a few days away. I am home, just like every day – or nearly – since I left the Élysée. The bay window is wide open, the sun warming the entire living room. I am working with my laptop on my knees. Earlier, I received a call from my former security officer who has an envelope to deliver. He arrives within half an hour. It is a beautiful bouquet of white and pink roses – exactly what I like. They are from François. He has not forgotten the date. This very morning he sent me a message: 'Nine years ago, the kiss in Limoges.'

Barring the pictures of the President with his helmet on, Julie Gayet, the statement, the whole mad situation, yes, it would have been our nine-year anniversary. But our relationship died before it turned nine. Still, if our love had a name that would be it: 'The Kiss in Limoges'. It is our very own legend. It was a Thursday, 14 April 2005. That date will always mean something to me.

Nine years later I agreed to go to dinner with him – for the second time since our separation – despite the fact that there was no anniversary left to celebrate. We spent the evening in an Italian restaurant in our neighbourhood, where we used to go when we lived together. The President and the First Lady were no more – no more grievances or recriminations, just a poignant mixture of joy and sadness. It felt like a huge waste. An irreparable waste. That evening, 279 Nigerian young women, aged twelve to seventeen, were kidnapped by the Islamist sect Boko Haram. We heard about it the following day.

François said he wished he had better protected our privacy. It certainly wasn't for want of trying on my part – I fought a losing battle to preserve our intimacy. With him, nothing and no one was off limits. Keeping people at a distance was not something he was good at.

I remember watching, aghast, as the President walked through our bedroom one evening with his PR adviser in tow. They were headed for the bathroom, which would have been turned into a makeshift meeting room had I not intervened. I threw the PR adviser out, outraged by such a lack of boundaries.

His security officers would also sometimes slip in between us and join in our conversation … I cannot remember how many times I had to ask them to give us a bit of space when we were out having a walk. It got to the point where I sometimes preferred to go home than have to put up with their presence. I even caught one of the croissant couriers sat on our bed, supposedly to fix the television channels.

When I reminded François during that bittersweet dinner that he always arbitrated against me when I tried to protect us, he admitted that he had been wrong. 'I should have listened to you and understood what mattered.'

But back to the kiss in Limoges – a long story I have to erase from my memory. It all started with a quarrel. One morning I found out that François Hollande and Nicolas Sarkozy were coming to *Paris-Match* to get their picture taken together for the cover of the magazine. They were also doing a joint interview ahead of the referendum on the European Constitution.

I was dumbfounded. No one had told me. More specifically, neither my editor-in-chief nor Hollande had breathed a word about it to me. I had heard that the latter was frustrated at me for not going on a business trip to Lebanon with him, but to do a photo and interview of such scope with the newspaper I worked for *without mentioning it to me* when we were so close was unthinkable!

Hollande's press officer called me: 'Valérie, what do you think you're doing making him do this? It's complete madness. A picture with Sarkozy, no less!'

I explained that I had absolutely nothing to do with it and had only just found out myself. She asked me to convince him to change his mind. I tried. But when I called him he sent me packing: 'You should have woken up earlier.'

For the life of me I could not fathom why he was reacting this way, and his strategy confused me even further. Appearing alongside his number one political rival would do him no favours – especially when those who opposed the European Treaty were already accusing him of colluding with him.

I packed up and left the magazine before he arrived. Tears clouded my vision as I sped down the motorway on my way home. I was baffled by my own tears. Were they the tears of a journalist who has just had her story 'stolen' or those of a woman who feels betrayed? Betrayal was already on the cards, even back then … I was still crying when I got home. I would later learn that François Hollande had asked for a tour of the magazine's offices, including the canteen – in hopes of bumping into me.

He tried to call me the next day but I hung up on him. This went on for several days. His press officer took over. I agreed to talk to her and I was stunned by how personal the conversation was.

'Valérie, have you still not noticed that Hollande is madly in love with you? Talk to him, I've never seen him this unhappy.'

I knew he was attracted to me, we had an undeniable

bond, a very special friendship, a bit too close, deliciously borderline at times. But love? No. It seemed absurd. Forbidden.

What she said came as a shock. I couldn't say a word. A week went by without any contact between him and me. The situation was becoming difficult to manage. I was on the brink of asking to be taken off coverage of the Socialist Party. In the end, though, I couldn't bring myself to do it. I eventually agreed to a reconciliatory lunch. We spoke for hours and he ended up missing the train he was supposed to take that afternoon.

One week later I agreed to accompany him on a business trip. The date was 14 April, the meeting was in Central France, near Châteauroux, I believe, though my recollection of the name of the town is blurry. We left Paris after lunch. I sat to his right in the backseat of the car. He wasn't his usual self, less jokey. There were silences between us and a certain gravitas. As François Hollande's loyal driver sped on, Hollande inched closer and took my hand. I was ill at ease but did not claim my hand back. A voice inside me whispered: 'You are mad. It's not too late to stop, take your hand back.' But I did nothing of the sort.

We talked and talked. Not about us. We talked politics, discussing the harm that the *Paris-Match* cover with Sarkozy had done. When we arrived we acted as if nothing had happened. Hollande's meeting went well, he was as bright and funny as usual. He argued in favour of a 'Yes' vote in the EU referendum. We were on the same page. I felt confident about the outcome at the polling stations in December, but he was sceptical.

That evening, Chirac appeared on a television show with young people in a bid to win them over to the European ideal. We watched the end of the show with a group of local elected representatives. It was a complete disaster: Chirac seemed completely out of touch with reality.

Afterwards, we got back on the road. My hotel was in Limoges. Hollande had to push on until Tulle. He took my hand in the car again. It took about an hour to get to Limoges. Hollande asked if I would come with him to Tulle. I said I couldn't, I had to leave very early the next morning for a meeting in Paris. Besides, I knew what 'come to Tulle with me' meant.

We weren't ready to say goodbye so we went to a café. He had a waffle and I had a *crêpe*, which we both washed down with a glass of wine. We spoke about our relationship for the first time. Our attraction to each other. It was all implied, nothing was said outright – as is his way. His tacit message was that he wasn't interested in a fling: he intimated that he had real feelings. I confessed I was hardly indifferent either, adding that a relationship was out of the question – it was too dangerous for both of us. Simply impossible. Neither of us were free.

He had to get back on the road to Tulle. We had to part
ways. At least, that was what was planned. When it came
to saying our goodbyes, everything between us changed
dramatically without either of us fully grasping what was
happening. What passed between us in that moment is
indescribable, it was like a scene from a film. A kiss like
no other kiss I'd ever shared with anyone. A kiss that had
been held back for nearly fifteen years, in the middle of
a crossroads.

François did not drive back to Tulle that evening. He
came with me to the station very early the next morning.
We had just experienced a unique moment – and yet I
struggled to call him by his first name or even simply to
use the familiar 'tu' when addressing him. A halo of modesty separated us once again.

*Port-au-Prince, Haiti, Tuesday 6 May 2014*
I woke up in a damp hotel room. I had only slept for a
few hours. I had arrived the previous day with a *Secours
populaire* delegation. The organisation's achievements
abroad rarely get the recognition they deserve so the idea
was to highlight its work in Haiti. When *Secours populaire* suggested the trip I was delighted. Delighted to be

out on the field again, and equally delighted to be given an opportunity to skip town. Being away from Paris on the two-year anniversary of the election could only be a good thing. (Two years already ... How time had flown!) I felt like a burns victim keen to avoid anything that reminded her of accident.

I agreed to a radio interview about *Secours populaire*'s work. But when the team set the date for Tuesday 6 May I failed to notice immediately that this was two years to the day after François had been elected. When I realised, two days before the interview, that it was a significant date I told him about it. He did not ask me to cancel or postpone it. Nor did he mention that he also planned to speak on *another radio station* that morning. I found out about it in a news report the next morning.

Once on the field, Paris was literally and figuratively miles away! Makeshift shelters crowded one another – tents and huts built from scrap, sheet metal and planks. Three hundred thousand Haitians still had nowhere to sleep since the earthquake. I did the interview at 4 a.m. Paris time. Stress started to build up ten minutes before it started. Someone offered me a rum to unwind, but I thought it would be wiser not to. I had decided what I would say the previous day and had prepared answers to the questions I imagined I would be asked. I suspected there would be a lot of personal questions.

The journalist started out by talking about Haiti. And after a few minutes, he slipped in some questions about François Hollande. I did not want to be ungracious and merely wished him luck for his three remaining years as President. I had no interest in spoiling this political anniversary or detracting from the aim of my visit, which was to help *Secours populaire*.

When I awoke a few hours later I checked the news reports, as I always did. I was astounded when I read François Hollande's statement about what the press was calling 'Gayetgate'. His answer to the question 'Did you behave honourably?' was: 'You cannot suggest here that I would have behaved dishonourably. I have never taken the easy way out, I have never behaved in a way that could cause embarrassment, I have never given in to vulgarity in any shape or form, I have never been coarse.'

François Hollande is a politician: he is fully in control of his rhetoric. He had carefully prepared that answer. His words had a devastating effect on me. Ever since we had separated three months earlier, he had been begging me to start over and resume our shared life. He had tried to see me. I had agreed. He had suggested dinner in that restaurant we liked. I had said yes.

For three months he had been harping on that he had made a mistake and had lost his way. He was forever repeating that I was the only one he loved and that he had barely seen Julie Gayet. A fortnight after the AFP statement, he told me he regretted our separation. Just four days previously he had mentioned the possibility of rekindling our relationship. He sent me flowers at every opportunity, including when I was abroad. He swore undying love. Some days it touched me. His renewed flame weakened my resolve. The door opened a crack and for a second I was tempted to give in again. But I quickly shut that door. I had regained my freedom and I relished it. I could not forgive him. The separation had been too dramatic.

Hearing him speak that way on the radio made those healing wounds on my heart bleed again. Perversely, the strength of the denial likened it to a confession. Not an ounce of regret transpired. He wanted me back but he was also stubbornly proud and incapable of expressing so much as a hint of remorse. A public apology was certainly not on the cards – no matter that he had promised me one. Merely saying my name in public was still difficult for him.

'Honourable'. That was the word he used. Where is the honour in the stolen pictures of a President on the back of a scooter? In a President who keeps his helmet on inside the building to avoid being recognised? Was his indifference honourable? Was it honourable to sideline me and send me away to hospital? Was there honour in sending orders from above to increase my daily dose of sedatives? Where is the dignity in the statement ordaining my repudiation, a cold decree dictated to an AFP journalist?

I DO NOT think he realised just how much damage his interview caused inside me. I was as stricken as on the darkest day of our separation. He plunged the blade in deeper still. Bitterness and anger made the wound fester.

I thought I had managed to piece myself back together over the past few months. Further denial hurt me to the core. There I was, in tears again, and in less than an hour I had to meet with the *Secours populaire* team to visit a school in Rivière froide. Having travelled to the other side of the world, I had managed to leave François behind for a while, but sadness had somehow caught up with me again.

I sent him a couple of text messages to get my anger off my chest. He was dumbfounded by my reaction and promised he would find the right words next time. Next time, always next time … I have lost count of the number of promises he has made and never held. Words clearly have no value for him.

That morning he lost me for good.

Once again I had to dry my tears, hide my pain and focus on what I had come to do in Haiti. My eyes were puffy when I went downstairs to meet the others. No matter, I could easily blame it on lack of sleep. And I had plenty of concealer to work with.

We drove down potholed roads for half an hour in a big SUV – destitution was everywhere we looked. At the end of a road that was really more of a trail, we finally reached the school financed by *Secours populaire* aid. The Haitian children transported me to a whole other world, miles away from the betrayals and pettiness of politics. All around me were people who did not have the luxury to think of anything other than survival. Our heartaches and my heartbreak paled in comparison to their poverty. After the earthquake, *Secours populaire* was able to build a school for 1,500 children. Those were the luckier ones. They were saved.

When we stopped at the drinking water treatment plant a group of street kids followed us. Some of them did not have shoes. They had no idea where I came from but they all wanted to hold my hand. For a moment, I forgot François. It was the children I was preoccupied with, those who would never be lucky enough to go to school. I thought, too, of my children, whom I had often left behind to go on assignments and trips. My boys, who paid the price for my complicated life. I felt so guilty!

Nine years earlier I had sacrificed my family for a man who had got rid of me at the first opportunity. Had I been able to resist that love my children would have had an anonymous and protected childhood. Where once I was madly in love, now I was just mad. No one had ever imagined he would one day become President. Not even me.

I felt like he had stolen everything from me. Nearly ten years of my life. Crossing the river exhausted me, I reached the other shore alone and covered in mud. How much longer would I feel sullied by all the qualifiers I had been saddled with: whore, the King's mistress, manipulative, hysterical and so on? I had never felt that I was being defended. The person I had given everything to never said a word or lifted a finger to shield and protect me. Instead he fanned the flames and abandoned me.

When I got back to Paris after Haiti I heard a very interesting radio show while I was driving: psychoanalysts were discussing introverts. One of them explained that it was a common mistake to confuse 'introverted' and 'shy'. An introvert is not afraid of other people, an introvert is someone who is unable to turn his feelings towards the outside, he keeps them inside, keeps them to himself. 'An introvert is sleek and smooth, shows no emotion. He wants to be more normal than the norm. It is a pathology.'

I pulled up to the kerb to jot down the last sentences. I

was stunned at just how well the description fitted François' inability to show what he feels in public. I have seen a man besotted with me make grand statements proclaiming his love, but the same man shied away from public demonstrations of affection. You really had to know him to understand that the more he joked, the more he was trying to hide a vexation.

I knew he was reluctant to talk about what is intimate, about truly personal things, and I hardly expected public introspection on the radio. I know he is simply incapable of such a thing. He could, however, have side-stepped the obstacle as he usually did; he is very good at being evasive. And he could have expressed regret. He chose instead to let his subconscious speak. He used the language of the powerful for whom anything goes and who does not owe a thing to anyone.

I wondered whether he was aware he had wreaked havoc. His lies stung deeply and destroyed the simple but essential feeling we call trust. My compass was broken because of it.

Since I have started writing I am flooded with memories every day. Today, I am remembering the day François was elected. That particular Sunday I was unable to embrace the joy that was all around us. He was intensely happy. I was not. I read in a beautiful book on Anne Pingeot – the woman François Mitterrand kept in the shadows, the woman who bore his illegitimate child – that on the day François Mitterrand was elected, she cried. She knew she was losing the man she loved. Oddly, when I recall that day, 6 May 2012, it is with Anne Pingeot that I identify, not Danielle Mitterrand – even though she was the woman who shared the President-elect's life that evening.

From politician to President – the change was almost instantaneous in François. Ahead of the results I barely managed to snatch thirty seconds for the two of us – to steal a brief kiss in the office of the Corrèze General Council. Then came that utterly surreal moment: the moment when the results were announced on television.

He had been elected.

François had become the President of France.

I could hardly believe it. I could see that his score had come as a bit of a blow. He remained impassive but under his mask I could sense slight disappointment. The two main TV channels were reporting different figures so he was preparing for the less favourable score. There was cause for celebration in any case: the whole Corrèze team was there and we opened a bottle of champagne.

He only took a sip and went straight back to work on his statement. Aquilino Morelle, who was to become his special adviser, looked over his shoulder as François redrafted. There he was, erasing all the work he had been given and starting from scratch – as he always did.

He was still rewriting his speech when I received a message from Nicolas Sarkozy's communications adviser saying that Sarkozy was trying to get in touch with François, whose mobile could not cope with the number of incoming calls. It was on my mobile that they ended up talking. I felt that that conversation should not be public so before handing my mobile to François I asked everyone to step outside. It did not go down very well with quite a few people.

Time was of the essence ... The crowd that had gathered on the Cathedral Square in Tulle had been waiting for several hours already. I asked François to take a minute for a few commemorative pictures as it was a unique moment. This irritated François, who sent me packing in no uncertain terms. His reaction took me aback. It should have been a moment of happiness and it had just been spoiled.

For me too, the tension had been very strong and was easing off. I broke down: I no longer felt able to go to the Cathedral Square. I locked myself up in the en suite bathroom and curled into myself on the cold tiles.

I tried to understand what I was experiencing. Evidently two strong feelings had just exploded when they came into contact with one another. I was happy for him – he had achieved his life's ambition but he was unable to share this emotion. If we could not be as one in moments like this, what would we ever be able to share?

At that very moment I sensed that things would never be the same again.

We had been so close, we had developed such a strong bond, but on his glory day I felt almost estranged from what he was experiencing. As I was going through all this in my head, someone came to bang on the door. Time to go. I hesitated, I thought of Cécilia Sarkozy, who was dragged to the Concorde on the evening her husband was elected – she had not wanted to go. Her reasons were different from mine. But the dizziness, the fear of what would unfold, was no doubt the same. How can you want that life – a life that will no longer belong to you?

I eventually came out of my makeshift refuge. I quickly reapplied my make-up and off we went. François did not talk to me in the car. He was like a man possessed by his speech – in a state of extreme concentration, as he always was before any major event. I respected those moments of silence. He retreated within himself. I knew better than to disturb him.

It was impossible to access the Cathedral Square, it was jam-packed. So many people had come! We continued on foot, pushing through the crowd. I was behind him, jostled this way and that. I kept being hit by cameras. The crowd went crazy when François walked up on stage. I stopped just beneath the stage. I had never followed him up on a platform, it had never felt like it was my place. After saying a few words he asked me to join him on stage. I was so unused to it that I did not move an inch, I was rooted to the spot. Arms pushed me towards the steps. François held his hand out to me. It was all completely new and I was touched by his gesture.

As Tulle is known for its accordion festival, the mayor had naturally planned accordion tunes. I had happened to mention one day that I loved 'La vie en rose' so the mayor surprised me with it. The crowd joined in and sang along while François led me into a couple of dance steps. I was both embarrassed and filled with joy. For me, *that* was an intense moment. It is still one of my favourite memories. I heard that 'real' Parisians – snobs – mocked the accordion atmosphere but the people of Corrèze were disappointed that the party did not last longer.

The picture of us dancing hangs in the President's Élysée office. There it remains, even after our separation. My own copy of the picture is still in my Élysée boxes – and those are still in my hall – but the image is imprinted on my memory.

I could hardly have imagined that the following week the daily *L'Express* would run the title 'Is Valérie Trierweiler trying too hard?' The editor-in-chief even claimed that I had requested 'La vie en rose' in Tulle on that victory day, and laboured his – outraged – point by labelling it a political act!

In spite of everything, that Tulle memory is one of my most treasured moments. I barely had time to tweet what I felt: 'So proud to be by the French President's side today and as happy as ever to be sharing François' life'. François was expected at the Place de la Bastille. The time had come to leave Tulle and head to Paris. He shook as many hands as he could before we were rushed to the Brive airport. How I would have loved to stay on the Cathedral Square, amid the quietly joyous crowd. The people of Tulle had been the first to pave his path to victory by welcoming him in their town thirty years earlier. It was real recognition – for him and for them.

We went back to the car and drove quickly to where the private plane awaited. It all looked like real life but it was interspersed with completely surreal elements. Messages started to come in from around the world. The man I had loved for so many years, the man no one believed in, had become Head of State. Angela Merkel, Barack Obama and many more proffered their congratulations. It was non-stop. Except when the signal eventually dropped – so it goes in Corrèze.

How long before the man by my side changed?

We joined the small team aboard the plane. A fortnight earlier, after the results of the first round came in, the whole team was able to relax a bit. Everyone was betting on the results of the second round. We all felt light and laid-back. Except François. The collective high spirits had spread to everyone but him. He had isolated himself but I do not think it was because he was afraid of losing. He was in the lead.

Having shared many other pre-vote anxieties, I knew full well that he would never take anything for granted until the final result came in. His anxiety when he waited for vote results was always all-encompassing and communicative. In any case, he contaminated *me* and I would become worse than him.

Not this time, though: we were confident. I wondered what he was thinking about at that moment. No doubt he was preparing his address to the crowd, but something else had taken over him, I could feel it. It was as if the weight of history had suddenly landed on his shoulders.

His reaction to victory on that second-round evening was altogether different to anything I had seen him go through previously. François took a flute of champagne but did not drink it.

Meanwhile, we rewrote history. Campaign anecdotes resurfaced. The flight flew by. Time was suspended. When we landed, a crowd had gathered around the airport to see the new President. He went to shake their hands – everything else would have to wait.

The crowd at the airport in Paris was much denser

than in Brive. The most impressive of all was the number of press motorcycles – too many to count. There could have been thirty or forty, who knows? They started chasing after our car that was headed to La Bastille. They looked like a swarm of bees. I feared for the safety of some motorcyclists who were prepared to take insane risks to capture an image of our car on the motorway or on the ring road.

I recalled footage of Jacques Chirac when he was elected. He pulled down the window of his car to wave, with his wife Bernadette by his side. It was as if I had suddenly realised what was happening. I was overcome by a rush of emotion and took François' hand. But calls and text messages were still coming in constantly and I did not manage to hold his hand for long … Our fingers separated… Until that moment, during all those years we had been together, as soon as we were next to one another we were incapable of keeping our hands off each other – we were like two magnets, always touching. This incredible event had disturbed our intimacy. From that moment, our tête-à-têtes started to become increasingly rare.

It was gone midnight when we reached La Bastille and it was then that I understood just how much things had changed. It was not a crowd but an ocean of human beings eagerly pressing against one another to get closer to François. Tens of thousands of people had turned out for him. We passed the VIP tent first, which was filled with all sorts of celebrities. Those who had been there from the outset and those who had 'just joined'. I did not know that Julie Gayet was already hanging around – like a snake in the grass. I did not see her coming. I had not bumped into her a single time during the campaign.

The first person I saw was my mother, who would not have missed this for the world. She was the person I went to embrace.

Just as so many other mothers fear for their children's wellbeing, she had sensed the potential danger of this particular situation. I read a mixture of pride and concern in her eyes. It was her very own daughter who was the President's partner: to say it had been unimaginable would be a major understatement. My northern *banlieue* of Angers was a distant memory, too distant…

FRANÇOIS WAS IN demand left, right and centre; the mêlée had reached mad levels. I eventually spotted my children, hiding in a corner to avoid pictures. I wondered what they were thinking. They certainly suspected that their lives too would be turned upside down but they could never have imagined that they would be treated as prey over the next twenty months – even after I left the Élysée, in fact. They could hardly have guessed that, instead of the privileges everyone imagines, people would constantly try to trap them and that fake stories would be made up to undermine me.

I spent a brief moment with them. No doubt, in their eyes, their mother was being monopolised by other people – my own sentiment in relation to François, as it happened.

The crowd was waiting to see François and hear his speech. He walked up on stage, as did I – everyone did. He delivered his speech in a hoarse voice: 'Thank you, French citizens, for making me President. I know what many of you feel: years of hurt, years of being scorned. We will have to repair, to recover, to reunite.' He spoke for twenty minutes. 'We are living a great moment, a victory that will make us happy.'

At the time I hardly registered what he was saying. The atmosphere was intoxicating. The crowd swayed and hooted with joy, it was all collective exhilaration and jubilation.

Suddenly, I saw that François was walking across the stage to the other end – even though I was by his side. I turned my head to observe what was going on. He walked all the way down the platform to kiss Ségolène Royal. I lost my composure, oblivious to the cameras zooming in on me, magnifying my crestfallen face on the giant screens. Was I the one who was ungenerous? Was I the insecure one – unsure of him? Did I still desperately crave legitimacy?

When he returned centre stage I whispered in his ear that I wanted him to kiss me, adding 'on the mouth'. Yes, I will admit I did want the difference to be clear. There had been a woman before, with whom he had four children, and there was another one now, with whom he lived. Not two women at the same time. I had had it with the infamous 'Hollande and his two women'. I felt reduced to nothing.

Not for a second did I imagine that the press would read those words on my lips – and publish them, presenting them as incriminating evidence in my trial as a 'dominating woman'. I experienced that as a violation. Not a scrap of intimacy was possible any longer. Everything would now be stolen – even a whisper in someone's ear...

I should have understood that this new world was not made for me. I am a spontaneous person, I have always been forthright, I say what I think – I am from a working-class background that hides nothing. The political elite is rather used to things being underhand; things are unspoken – you greet those you despise with a wide smile and malign them behind their back. I was ill-prepared for this life, and for that I paid the price.

I was head over heels in love with a man who no longer wanted to invest as much in our relationship as he had done until then. Success was driving the man I was madly in love with away from me. My world had been turned on its head.

The man who had wanted me so much for so many long years had become the French President and, simultaneously, a different person. It was inevitable. François compartmentalised everything, I sensed that he did not want me to be a part of his political career anymore and was suddenly keeping me at arm's length. I thought I could withstand just about anything from him, but his indifference was more than I could bear. All women need the men they love to see them. I am just like any other woman.

It was in that context that I found myself being 'parachuted' into the role of First Lady – an ill-defined role without an official status – when I had wanted to continue to lead my own life, independently. I would need to adapt to that stranglehold but I had not yet understood that. I was not sure how we would strike our new balance, or whether we would even manage it.

When I worked as a political journalist François and I would spend hours upon hours discussing our common passion. For years we shared everything. Politics is a central part of my life too. In fact, politics brought us together, well before we fell in love.

Once we got to the Élysée, I had to wrench myself away from that part of him and it was heart-rending. I made sure not to encroach upon what was political. Figuratively and literally, I did not step outside the boundaries that had been drawn for me. I never put a foot through the door to power. I did not even know where the advisers' offices were. I called the door separating 'the Madame wing' from the rest of the Palace the 'Berlin Wall'. Within those walls, you don't say the 'Élysée' but the 'Palace'. Personally, I never could call it that. I only ever attended one meeting with advisers on the other side: we were preparing for International Women's Day. Everyone said my ideas for 8 March were excellent. Not a single one was implemented.

It was during the campaign that uneasiness crept in. I struggled to find my place in François' campaign from the very start. I began to put on weight, my neck was tense and would often freeze up. My whole face was tense, and covered in eczema. The stress was palpable, I felt like I had aged considerably in just a few months. A campaign can be an unimaginable shock, it is difficult to imagine what it is like to be constantly assaulted by cameras when you are not prepared for it.

Why was I having such trouble adapting to all this? I blamed myself for not being stronger. Now I understand why I wasn't. Ever since he had begun campaigning,

François put me in a constant state of insecurity with his lies; he was secretive and cagey. He was unable to give me a clear picture of just how much distance he wanted to instil between us on certain topics. Instead, he did it his way – don't ask, don't tell – he lied by omission, lied full stop and avoided certain topics. If I had a penny for every time I heard something from his 'gang' that he should really have told me himself…

Sometimes I would disappear, to get back on my feet and rebuild my self-confidence.

We were a couple but we were hardly facing a normal situation: we were en route to the Presidency. I thought we had a solid bond, I thought we were inseparable – as we had been during all the years leading up to this, when he was in the political wilderness. But since his career had taken off, our closeness was slowly eroding. He had other horizons on his mind. He barely saw me anymore. In contrast, he was the only person who mattered to me. His victory wasn't what counted. To me, there was only him, the love of my life.

Back to the election victory celebrations… The Minister of the Interior was worried things might get out of hand as the crowd around Place de la Bastille was already getting a bit rowdy, so our departure was moved forward. We went back to our home on rue Cauchy. On the return journey, cars honked all the way. François had his window down and waved. We were still being chased by a horde of press motorcycles. It was utter madness at the foot of our building. Several dozens of journalists and photographers crowded the street; TV crews were filming live. Life as we knew it, our life, was about to change drastically. It was as if I was a spectator, not a protagonist, in my own life. Looking from the outside in.

François' crazy race did not let up. The next day he ran from meeting to meeting to prepare his Cabinet. He shared with me the name of the future Prime Minister as well as a few ministers. But thanks to my experience as a political journalist I knew that lists continually change until the very last minute. All I did was suggest a name, which in the event did not sit well with François. I had thought the editor-in-chief of *Elle* magazine would be a good fit for the ministry of Women's Rights. François' reply was: 'I can't do that to Giesbert.' Franz-Olivier Giesbert, the then director of the weekly magazine *Le Point*, was the life partner of *Elle*'s editor-in-chief. François had first-hand experience of his partner being promoted instead of him, and in his mind, Franz-Olivier Giesbert could only have seen his partner's nomination as a personal snub. Macho solidarity at its basest.

I did criticise a few names he was toying with but it

certainly had no influence on who he chose. As a matter of fact, I did not know half of the potential ministers. They had emerged from the depths of the Socialist Party, the Radicals and the Greens. Their nomination resulted from pre-electoral agreements, a bit of pot luck too. Worse, some of the women were even chosen from a catalogue.

Unsurprisingly, the press wrote – with that air of authority it always assumes – that we had drafted the list together. It was of course utter nonsense – François is not easily influenced.

Once we got home to rue Cauchy, François continued to call various people. I warned him several times that when he was on the balcony I could hear his conversations through the window in our room. The neighbours could listen in too if they pricked up their ears.

Security services came to do a thorough search of the flat, check that bugs had not been planted and that the new President was not in any danger. The bay window was a security risk. Several flats overlooked the inside of our flat and security recommended having bullet-proof windows fitted.

It would have cost tens of thousands of euros and François refused to do it because it did not fit in with his 'President Normal' agenda. Besides, there was hardly any point as the President spent time a lot of time on the balcony – we had lunch or dinner on it whenever the weather allowed. In the end, our security protocol was fairly basic: two emergency alarms were fitted, one in the entrance and one in our room – directly linked to the President's security officers, with a password to alert them to a very serious danger, in case we had a gun to our heads. Every single contingency was catered for, including the very worst.

François wanted to lighten the whole security apparatus. He got rid of the CRS[12] van stationed in front of the building and of the police officer who stood guard 24/7 on our floor. He also put an end to routine ID checks on anyone entering the building.

When we were in our flat on rue Cauchy we could have been mistaken for a normal couple, if it weren't for the crowd of waiting journalists every morning on the sidewalk, questions at the ready. They were spot on: he never shot them down, every morning before he left he took the time to answer.

After the madness of the last month of campaigning, I was glad to spend some time with my son, who was studying for his baccalaureate. He had to take his sports exam a few days after the election. On the morning of the exam he looked out the window, saw the cameras and

---

12 French riot control forces.

had a panic attack. He was simply unable to leave the flat. I begged him to go to his exam but he was rooted to the spot.

I tweeted, asking the journalists and photographers to respect our privacy, to leave us alone. My request was interpreted as an affront: how could I, a journalist, reject my own colleagues? I could hardly tell them that my son hadn't slept a wink and was in no state to go to a baccalaureate exam because of them!

I managed to reassure him and convince him to go. But when the examiner saw him arrive in such low spirits he sent him home and gave him a new exam date.

Every day I was made increasingly aware of the fact that our daily life would never be the same again.

The next day my son announced that he wanted to live somewhere else, that he could not stand the pressure any longer. Within twenty-four hours I found some friends who agreed to let him live in their studio. I was devastated to see him go while he was in the middle of sitting his exams.

One more crack had appeared – and it was only day two after the election.

Inauguration day was approaching. François' team had contacted Nicolas Sarkozy's team to prep the transition. I followed from afar. I received a text message from Carla Bruni-Sarkozy asking me if I would keep the personal service team: they were 'wonderful people – with them you needn't bother twirling your spoon in your coffee'. I explained that we did not plan on keeping the Élysée fully staffed: it was not François Hollande's style and did not fit with his vision. Much less mine. In any event, Carla and I agreed to see each other during the traditional talk between the two Presidents in the handover of power – to discuss housekeeping matters together.

THE GUEST LIST had to be drawn up for the presidential inauguration. François wanted to avoid a repeat of Nicolas Sarkozy's inauguration – the blended family treading the red carpet rolled out across the *Cour d'honneur*. As a result, François did not want his children or mine to attend. He did not even want his father to be there.

He organised a dinner with his four children – and asked me not to be there – so he could explain his decision to them in person and address the delicate matter of Ségolène Royal's presence: she was both a female front-runner in politics and his former partner. Her presence would be interpreted on a personal level no matter what, and François did not want to enter the Élysée regally, mixing public and private life – ironic as that may now seem.

The decision not to invite his family was his, not mine.

I told him it struck me as rather cruel for his children. Meanwhile, I did not dare invite my mother, who would have loved to be there.

People simply could not understand why Ségolène Royal and her children were not at François Hollande's inauguration. His children knew what was what but the press blamed his decision on me. Article after article accused me of attempting to sideline the mother of the President's children. No one seemed to notice that neither my children nor my family were there either. Not that François ever spoke up to defend me and own up to the fact that it was his own decision – a decision he made on principle.

Every step of the way, another chapter of the media novel was penned – based on erroneous interpretations and misunderstandings. That sum of minor discrepancies between reality and fiction created a media monster that was out of control. By dint of repetition, the media fiction ended up becoming the truth in people's mind. The press authored a novel with a character who was supposed to be me. I, however, did not recognise that fictional version of me in the slightest.

But the First Lady has no right to speak in public or defend herself.

I met the protocol team and was given a detailed run-through of François' inauguration day – complete with print-outs. Everything would be timed, carefully designed and prepared. I began to grasp just how out of the ordinary this event was. The stress started to build up inside me.

It was the eve before the big day. François and I barely saw each other. François was still caught up in the throes of politics. Everything was happening in fast forward; he had dozens of decisions to make each day.

My preoccupations were certainly lighter – my outfit, for example. I wanted it to be sober. I had never worn haute couture and, even though France is home to a flurry of couture houses, it never occurred to me to knock on their doors.

Amor, the stylist who had been dressing me for television, still gave me advice for free. On this occasion too, he helped me. We chose a Georges Rech dress – a designer label I was used to wearing. The dress needed alterations – sleeves were added and it was lengthened. I had a dress fitting the evening before the inauguration and it did not hang the way I wanted. There was very little time for more alternations but Amor promised it would be ready in time for the next morning.

It was not a restful night and we did not get much sleep. François was to be officially sworn in seventh President of the Fifth Republic. In the morning we each got ready in separate rooms. We both went through the hands of a stylist, a make-up artist and a hairdresser as if we were going to the town hall to be married. We had already been asked hundreds of times whether we were going to get married. Frankly, I had the feeling that what we were about to experience was going to be much more intense than going to the town hall. I felt completely in sync with him, I could never have imagined in a million years what would happen nineteen months later. It was unthinkable after everything we had lived through together. We were inseparable.

I had to leave a few minutes ahead of him and appeared in front of him, dressed and ready. He complimented me and I knew he was being sincere: a woman in love knows when she is able to surprise the man she loves. François looked at me with shiny eyes. The only thing he disapproved of was the height of my heels – he could not stand me being taller than him. One last kiss and I left the flat. We had always known how to communicate more with our eyes than with words. We communicated through gestures, too. When he took my hand and squeezed it, I knew what it meant.

I took a seat in the back of 'my' new car. From that point onwards, I would be flanked with a driver and two security officers – two duos alternated every other week – everywhere I went. There are no words to describe what I felt when the car went through the gates of the Élysée Palace. I had often been there as a journalist.

None of it had hit home yet. I could not get used to the idea that I was the First Lady of France. The First Lady's role is to project a certain image of France, to represent France, but she has no official status. It is such a strange role, but it matters in the eyes of the French people. Many did not recognise me as the First Lady because François and I were not married. Subconsciously, I probably took that on board.

The sheer mass of photographers was mind-blowing. As I took my first steps on the red carpet I could hear my name being called from all sides: 'Valérie' and 'Madame Trierweiler'. I was nervous but I managed to smile. Posing for the cameras is not something that comes easily to me, I struggle to look natural. I don't enjoy it, it is not my strong point.

I recognised a few familiar faces among the photographers. In a twenty-year career at *Paris-Match*, I had met a lot of photographers and even worked with some of those who were at the inauguration. But this time it was a different matter entirely. They were not interested in their colleague the journalist. It was François Hollande's partner they wanted: the First Lady.

I was barely aware of what was happening as I took my first steps as the new First Lady of France. The images would become part of history: for decades, at each new election, the TV footage would be playing in a loop. I was overcome with emotion when I saw François' car arrive – when I heard the sound of the gravel under the tyres. He was a different man in my eyes.

Nicolas Sarkozy welcomed him, while Carla greeted me. The two men, who had known each other for years, walked up to the President's office for the official hand-over of power, the transmission of nuclear launch codes and of sensitive dossiers. François would later tell me that the exchange from head of state to head of state was extremely brief. Most of that conversation remained private. Nicolas Sarkozy shared with him just how painful his five-year term had been for Carla, how she had struggled with the excessive media scrutiny and scandal-mongering. He confessed that he had called on specialist companies to increase the visibility of honourable mentions and positive articles about Carla; he had been forced to use search engine optimisation to shield his wife from the nastiness that was circulating on the internet.

While the two men talked, Carla showed me around the 'Madame wing', which would become my own. A sumptuous office, called the Fougères living room,[13] awaited me. It had a view on the Élysée gardens, and used to be Caroline Murat's room – better known as Caroline Bonaparte, a younger sister of Napoleon Bon-

---

13  Fern living room.

aparte. The office was spacious, light and feminine with its flowery hangings. On one wall hung a portrait of Louis XV. Two paintings by Hubert Robert, an eighteenth-century painter, hung on the wall opposite – I later learned that the paintings used to decorate François Mitterrand's room. Cécilia Sarkozy had turned that living room into an office before her divorce from Nicolas Sarkozy. Bernadette Chirac had chosen a darker room, with a view on the Faubourg Saint-Honoré. It was the one my Chief of Staff Patrice Biancone – the only person I asked to recruit – eventually chose. Carla explained that she had only been in this office a couple of times. We sat down in the living room next door, which one of my sons would call the Gaddafi living room because of the green sofas and hangings.

Carla and I had a frank and sincere discussion. I felt no animosity towards her. Quite the contrary. I had bought her first album when it came out and my ex-husband used to listen to it on repeat. During the campaign months, without having met, she and I had both adopted a non-aggression pact. I strongly feel that women and children should be spared in political jousts, just like in times of war. Carla Bruni-Sarkozy has never spoken ill of me in public and I have never criticised her either.

She explained how trying her husband's mandate had been. There were tears in her eyes: 'I shouldn't say it, but I am happy all this is over. It will be easier for you because journalists are your friends.' I replied that unfortunately things would probably not be as simple as that.

'I am worried that without politics my husband will lose his meaning in life,' she said.

At that point, I had known Nicolas Sarkozy for over two decades. I first interviewed him in the '90s and bumped into him again very often after that. The last time I had seen him was shortly after he was elected President, in June 2007. Governor General Michaëlle Jean was visiting a Canadian cemetery in Normandy, along with the Canadian delegation, and I was covering the event for *Paris-Match*. When Nicolas Sarkozy arrived, he welcomed each member of the delegation personally. I was greeted with: 'How are you? Have you solved your problems?'

At the time, it was a poorly kept media secret that I was living with François. Following Nicolas Sarkozy's victory, Ségolène Royal had made an AFP statement that acknowledged the situation: 'I have asked François Hollande to leave the family home.'

I responded respectfully: 'All is well, thank you, Mr President.' He took the fact that I used the formal 'vous' for a mark of defiance. I was merely respecting both protocol and his new status as President of the Republic. He insisted on addressing me with the informal 'tu', but I kept my responses sober and polite.

Sometime later I felt it was safe to attend the President's New Year Wishes to the press – a yearly ritual for French presidents. It was January 2008, my relationship with François Hollande was now out in the open – we had been together for over two years but we had kept it under wraps until after the outcome of the presidential elections, mostly for Ségolène Royal's sake. It was no longer a secret for anyone. I looked on as several of my notoriously left-wing colleagues elbowed each other to shake Nicolas Sarkozy's hand. I was not one of them.

Later, as Sarkozy was heading to his office, he spotted me waiting to get my coat back from the cloakroom and whispered in my ear: 'I saw some pretty nice pictures of you in *Voici*.'

So the President had time to read glossy gossip magazines … François and I had indeed been papped during a romantic New Year's break on a small island in Thailand.

This anecdote illustrates my familiarity with 'Sarkozy, the political animal'. So when Carla shared her fear that her husband might be losing his meaning in life, I answered: 'I am not going to tell you who your husband is but I know high-level politicians – I live with one of them. Those men will never be able to quit politics.'

I have always been convinced – back then, as I am now – that in spite of what he said, Sarkozy would be a candidate in 2017. He will want his return match.

Carla and I continued chatting, as two friends might. She shared the small victory it had been to finally fit into the trouser suit she was wearing that day, as she was struggling to lose her pregnancy weight. She also told me how much she had suffered from the attacks against her on the internet. Several times over the course of our conversation she was teary-eyed. I asked her to show me pictures of her children.

Time flew by. We spent thirty-eight minutes together and we could have talked for longer but José – the Chief of Protocol who would advise me on etiquette, as he had done for Bernadette Chirac, Cécilia Sarkozy and Carla Bruni-Sarkozy – came in to inform us that the two Presidents had finished their talk.

We went to meet the two men in the Hall. Sarkozy said a few polite words to me, using the formal 'vous'. He too told me how hard it was on the family. And then, there we were, the four of us on the front steps of the Élysée Palace. Naturally I kissed Carla on the cheek. François shook hands with both of them.

He did not walk the now former President to his car. This potential affront to his predecessor was later much discussed and publicised. But I knew François. He was simply not fully familiar with the rules of *savoir vivre* – it would take time for him to get used to protocol. And he was in a hurry. Very much in a hurry to get to the next part: his official inauguration. In fact he turned on his heels without waiting for me either.

We headed to the Hall of Festivities, where François' inauguration was to take place. As part of the new President's swearing in, the President of the Constitutional Council places the Collar of the Grand Master of the Legion of Honour around his neck.

I stood to François' right, behind him. I could not concentrate on his speech, which I had not read beforehand. In the pictures I appear to be gazing into space – everything still seemed so surreal to me. I can now recall a few sentences from his speech: two years later as they echo in my mind, they have a different ring altogether. 'Confidence is about setting the example.' And 'State power will be exercised with dignity.'

At that moment, François impressed me. He seemed strong and wilful. He was in his role, in his function, wearing the costume. I was proud to be by his side, proud to see the man I loved meet his destiny, even though no one had believed he would.

After his speech, François went to greet the constitutional bodies and the guests. The Chief of Protocol signalled that I should follow him. I did as he did and shook outreached hands. Most of the faces were familiar – I had met these men and women through work – and there were even people who were close to me.

Unbeknown to me, I had committed a crime! That very evening, the press and some of the President's advisers rebuked me for having dared to greet these constitutional bodies, leaders and representatives of all the French institutions. I read that it wasn't my role. It had never been done, apparently. I had followed the Chief of Protocol's lead. But I had not followed all the rules of etiquette, because I did not know them all. To say hello and shake hands seemed more polite than not to do so.

Élysée customs were to remain impenetrable to me, especially meeting and greeting: when I did not shake hands, I was criticised for being cold and haughty; when I did, I was given bad press for thinking too highly of myself. I could not win. Eventually, I took to standing a couple of metres behind François and greeting people with a mere nod, sometimes a smile.

François' inauguration day was jam-packed. It was a cloudy day and rain started pouring down just before François' parade on the Champs-Élysées. The car had been ordered especially, a Citroën DS5 hybrid with a sun-roof, and François absolutely refused to take an umbrella.

I left a few minutes before him to wait for him at the top of the Champs-Élysées. In spite of the downpour, seeing him drive up the avenue was an indescribably intense moment. It echoed so many other mythical images.

The rain was beating down and it was very windy, I

was shivering, trying to shelter myself as best I could under the Arc de Triomphe. The wind kept lifting my wrap dress so that I had to hold it down to avoid giving the photographers an eyeful. (They did manage to get a shot eventually – at the Jules Ferry homage, by the monument dedicated to his memory in the Tuileries gardens.)

After the ceremony under the Arc de Triomphe, the new President went to wave to the crowd. The Chief of Protocol had decided we would then drive down the Champs-Élysées from one end to the other in François' car. I did not know what to do when François went off to shake some hands without waiting for me. Should I follow him? Should I stand out in the cold looking like an idiot?

François' car followed him as he paced down the Champs-Élysées shaking hands. No one told me what to do. I tried to catch up with the Citroën DS5 as I would have been left behind if not… The critics were right, I clearly influenced the President's every move…

Once we got back to the Élysée, I had to insist for ten minutes before François would agree to change into a new suit before lunch. To say that he was soaked would be an understatement. He grumbled and it was only when I pointed out that it would be a shame for him to be ill at the very start of his presidential mandate that he finally heeded my suggestion.

We were in a room near the Portrait Room, where the lunch was meant to be held and the former socialist prime ministers and their spouses were expecting us. It had been my idea to organise this get-together. It was my only contribution to the organisation of François' inauguration day.

François had initially thought of inviting his loyal gang of 'Hollandaise' followers. Naturally his few early-day supporters deserved to be there. But I warned him that inviting just his entourage would contradict his electoral promise to bring about a 'kinder, gentler, more inclusive France' and might project a 'cliquey' image of the new President.

Next came the two tribute ceremonies – for Jules Ferry, then for Pierre and Marie Curie – but the inauguration day wasn't over yet. The last item on the agenda was the President-elect's welcome at the Paris Town Hall. It was incredibly moving. The huge crowd on Place de l'Hôtel-de-Ville was warm and welcoming. Granted, there was something grotesque about the whole situation: François Hollande and the Mayor of Paris in two huge grandiose armchairs, looking more regal than republican – and the Deputy Mayor and me sat behind them … But there were so many friendly faces!

When we left, Jean-Marc Ayrault told me how happy he was to become Prime Minister. It was not official yet but it was an open secret. François had not hesitated for a second, he had made his choice a long time ago. He appreciated his loyalty and did not want to be in anyone's shadow. Ayrault fitted the bill perfectly.

Everything was timed to the minute. We returned to the Élysée and finally got a chance to visit properly. I discovered the President's office, which I had never seen during my seventeen years of political journalism. I had been into the adjacent green living room, which used to be Jacques Attali's office when he was François Mitterrand's adviser. Jacques Chirac used to hold 'off-the-record' briefings in that 'green room'. I had been to a few of those meetings, generally ahead of state visits. But walking into the President's office with François was far more emotional.

We visited a few other offices. Then we were led to our private apartment. Carla had told me: 'You'll love it, I had the whole place redone.' It was a sumptuous apartment – at once spacious and impersonal. In any case we planned to continue to live in our own flat on rue Cauchy. In fact, I returned to our flat that very evening – as soon as I had met the Élysée maîtres d'. I was alone that evening as François had gone to Berlin, to have dinner with the German Chancellor.

I got home in a state of exhaustion and feverish excitement at the same time. I switched the television on but couldn't concentrate and kept channel-hopping. Flashes of the unbelievable day we had just had were running through my mind.

Then I heard that François' plane had been hit by lightning and had had to change its route and land in Paris. François had been forced to board another Falcon to continue his journey. I felt like I too had been hit by thunder: I had not heard from him. Five minutes later I got a call from the Secretary General of the Élysée. We barely knew each other but I got a good vibe from him. He told me that François was well.

I was not. I could not understand why François had not called me to reassure me. Not even a text message. Would there now be filters between us instead of a direct link? Would he always be so absorbed by his new life that he could not spare a thought for me? How could he not know how much I would worry when I heard about the incident?

Luckily I had planned to spend the evening with friends – I did not want to spend the evening alone after such an extraordinary day. There were about ten of us and we danced and partied. It was my hen party, except that it was my life as a free woman we were bidding goodbye to, rather than my single life. In the company of friends, the tension that had built up during the day dissolved.

In the end, François and I both got home more or

less at the same time, around 2 a.m. He briefly delivered his first impressions on Angela Merkel and told me he had not wanted to worry me unnecessarily by mentioning the plane incident. I knew we were both thinking about the same thing: a fright we had had together during the 2004 regional elections campaign. At the time, I was just a journalist accompanying the First Secretary of the Socialist Party. We flew to Brittany in a flimsy little plane – the very definition of what you might call an old crate. The weather conditions were extremely unfavourable and the closer we got to our destination, the stronger the wind blew. The pilot was reluctant to land – the cabin was being badly shaken as it was. François encouraged him to take the risk. It occurred to me that we could die.

We have talked about that day many times since, about how we could have died together without ever having loved one another. We spoke of it again, at 2 a.m., on the night after François' swearing in. François and I did not see death the same way: he feared it above all else. He is one of those men who build themselves a destiny precisely in an attempt to escape the fate that awaits every man. To leave a mark, to survive one way or another. To make it into books and to make history. It was his personal quest for immortality. He refused to talk about death, he did not know how to behave around dying people and the terminally ill. They scared him and he avoided them. He also avoided people who were going through personal tragedies, as though grief were a contagious disease.

I became aware of this when we found out about his mother's serious illness, during the 2007 campaign: he asked me to call her to see how she was. He could not deal with hearing the news first-hand, he was unable to face it head on.

When he asked me that, I had not yet met his mother, Nicole; I had only spoken to her on the phone. A few years earlier I had been assigned to write a profile of François for *Paris-Match*. Her son had told her I could be trusted, so she had agreed to speak to me. Things got off to a good start between us and she opened up to me. I remember writing in my profile of François Hollande that he was 'abnormally normal'…

In 2006, he had asked me to call his mother a second time … to tell her about our romantic involvement. He did not feel up to doing it himself. This sort of announcement is an important moment in a person's lifetime. It went well: Nicole was happy to hear that her son was happy, especially as her own relationship with Ségolène Royal had hardly been plain sailing over the years.

I called Nicole nearly every day throughout the 2007 campaign.

I met François' parents over the summer of 2007. They welcomed me with open arms. We also went to visit them for the weekend in Cannes. But Nicole's illness kept progressing and the more her health deteriorated, the more François struggled to talk to her directly. The end of her life was terrible. There was nothing to do but to wait for the fatal outcome.

After a long stay at the clinic, Nicole was eventually discharged and cared for by a nurse at her home. Philippe, François' eldest brother, spent his nights at her bedside. We took over on the weekends, though it was very little compared to what Philippe did during the week. We stayed in the same room as Nicole at night, by her side. It was impossible to sleep – we could hear her death rattles and spent the night wondering whether she might be breathing her last breath. To François, touching the body that had carried him was unthinkable, but his mother's skin was very dry and cracked. He asked me to apply moisturising cream as decency prevented him from doing it himself. I did it. I was touched and surprised by his gratitude: 'I will never leave you, you are so kind to my mother,' he said. It is natural to care for your mother-in-law if you love her son, as the bond that ties them together is so strong.

The call we were dreading from Philippe came on a weekday. He asked us to come as quickly as we could. He was convinced that the end was near. As I remember it, it was a Wednesday. François had some commitments and wanted to wait until Saturday and convince his children to pay a last visit to their grandmother. Two of them agreed on the condition that I would not be there. Their parents' official separation was only a few months old and the wound was still raw. I took a step back to give them the space they needed

On the morning the three of them had planned to leave, the phone rang very early. Nicole had passed away. Philippe and François both cried on the phone. The children cancelled their trip and in the end I was the one who went with François so that he could see the body of the mother he loved so dearly.

The cremation took place three days later but I was not allowed to attend because the children would be there.

I will never forget François' face when he returned to rue Cauchy... He had warned me that he would be bringing his mother's ashes back to Paris for the funeral. I bought five bouquets of white flowers and placed them on top of the chest of drawers Nicole had given us, along with a picture of her. It was a sort of altar for her ashes, until the service two days later.

François rang the doorbell. The box containing the ashes was in a supermarket plastic bag. I cannot begin to describe the expression on his face. I have never seen it on anyone else. Distraught is far too weak a word. He was in shock, traumatised, devastated. He was moved by the flowers.

The next day we went to organise the funeral together. We met the priest and saw where she would be buried in the Saint-Ouen cemetery. I still did not know whether I would be allowed to attend the service. Until now his children had consistently refused to meet me.

I was so worried that I would be cast aside, that I would not be allowed to share this moment with him, that I could not bear the thought of asking François directly. Eventually I was forced to bring it up, as he had not. As was often the case, he preferred things to remain unspoken. When I asked him, he said that in his mind it went without saying that I should be there.

Notwithstanding, my attendance at the service continued to be problematic for the children. Until the last minute we were not certain whether they would be there. When we entered the church, François said: 'The family will sit here, on the left. You sit on the other side.'

So a couple was not 'family'. I took it on the chin – it was his mother's funeral, I had no right to make his life difficult on such a day. And so I found myself sitting alone on the right-hand side of the church.

After the service, he went to wait for his children outside the church. I do not know exactly what happened. He eventually returned, with his four children in tow.

He was joyful and grief-stricken all at once. Immensely sad about his mother and incredibly happy that his children were there, that they agreed to enter the church even though I was there.

After the ceremony, he ignored me and did not introduce his children to me. I took the initiative of greeting them myself and they did not reject me. The eldest of his daughters even came for lunch at rue Cauchy with the rest of François' family – cousins I had not yet met. That mournful day marked the beginning of the normalisation of our situation.

In those days of grieving, François' pain touched me. As a mother to three boys I was deeply moved to see a 57-year-old man so affected by the death of his mother. I also guessed that he would now feel relieved of the burden of his mother's judgement, which he had always feared. He would no longer need to seek her approval.

She had loved him so! No one had ever held out such a flattering mirror for him. Death pushes everyone to the front line – we stand alone to face our fate. It is a violent uprooting but it also frees you.

On the day François was elected, it was Nicole he thought of, first and foremost. I sensed it so I bought flowers and set aside an hour in his agenda – with his secretary acting as my accomplice. We went to the cemetery early in the morning – there was not a paparazzo in sight to ruin the moment. As always when we went to the cemetery, I let him have a moment alone at his mother's graveside. She was the person who had given life to him, and so much more. The person who had given him his joie de vivre.

What was going through his mind in that moment – a moment that is unlike any other? No doubt he thought about everything he owed to her. About how he missed her presence and support in this turning point in his life, this moment when his life and his fate collided.

I remember the long conversations François and I used to have when Nicole first got ill. We would talk about everything Nicole wanted for us. She had said something lovely about us: 'I have had to wait for both of my sons to be over fifty to see them so deeply in love.'

At that time Philippe had also started over, with Caroline. Just before she passed away, Nicole said: 'I can die happy, since both of my sons are happy.'

On the day of his inauguration, François' thoughts went out to his mother again.

After the madness of the inauguration, we both needed to get some sleep. Since the first round of the presidential elections we had slept very little: the days were jam-packed so that fatigue had built up for both of us, not to mention our nights of insomnia, which rarely coincided.

François had been waking up in the night every single night since the Socialist primaries. His sleep pattern was completely skewed. François does not let anyone see what haunts him, but at night it takes over. The fear of losing, mainly. The burden and responsibilities if he did become President. He knew that any external event could be a game-changer. Until D-day nothing was a given.

## Late May 2014

A dismal 3 per cent of voters say they would vote for François Hollande if he were to run again in 2017. He has become a laughing stock once more, just as he was four years ago. I am pained to witness such an incredible waste, angry at that self-sabotage. Obviously in a private capacity but also as a Socialist Party voter. How could he have reached that low point? How could he have fallen to 3 per cent again? Memories flood me, like bubbles rising up to the surface.

Back to square one: when he was preparing to become a candidate in the presidential election and nobody had any faith in him. He was the only one who believed he could pull it off. As for me, I was prepared to follow him to the end of the world and back. It all began one morning in November 2010. While he was getting dressed in our room, he mentioned running for President.

It was not a subject we had previously discussed. I knew it was his goal and that was how we would sometimes broach it, with that euphemism, 'the goal'. We had never spelled it out, we had never spoken the words 'presidential election'. He veiled his ambition in modesty. We had only lifted the taboo once, as he drove us past rue du Faubourg Saint-Honoré in my car. 'Look, we're driving past home' he said as we passed the Élysée Palace. It certainly came as a surprise, and I roared with laughter. He had always known how to make me laugh. No subject was too serious to joke about, including himself – he was a genius at self-deprecation.

That November morning was altogether different: there was not a hint of sarcasm in his eyes. He was serious and he asked me for the first time what I thought: 'After what happened in 2002 and 2007, you cannot afford to get it wrong. If Ségolène Royal's defeat has taught us anything it is that you have only one question to ask yourself. Either you think you are the best and you go for it, or you don't and you let somebody else stand.' He did not hesitate for one second before answering: 'I am the best.'

'In that case,' I said, 'put your money where your mouth is.'

We continued to talk. He had no doubts about his

abilities. He was always convinced that he would prevail over Dominique Strauss-Kahn, who at the time was a Socialist Party candidate and was leading in the polls by a long way. François was convinced that Ségolène Royal would not run if he did. He had let her have her go in 2007 and this time it was his turn.

He had been preparing his candidacy with the utmost discretion. He had started from the very bottom of the pecking order. In 2008, following the disastrous Reims Congress, François was completely discredited. Ségolène Royal was blaming him for her defeat in the presidential elections. Any debacle calls for a scapegoat and this time it had landed on him. Everyone wanted to turn the Hollande page and move on to a new chapter. Eleven years of him leading the Socialist Party was more than enough!

Just before the Reims Congress I decided to do something for him, for us: I bought a new car. I swapped my old Clio for a Renault Mégane. I went to the car dealer to get a new car straight away. I did not choose the colour, I took what they had in stock – I would have been more particular if I had been buying a pair of shoes.

I had a plan. I wanted him to hold his head up high as he stood down as First Secretary of the Socialist Party. I wanted us to be seen leaving together in my new car – symbolising a new life, a new start. Basically I wanted him to publicly own up to our relationship.

At the last moment, he refused to do it. François' succession was a failure, marred by in-fighting. The run-off between the contenders to take the helm of the Socialist Party was turning into a psychodrama – Martine Aubry, Bertrand Delanoë and Ségolène Royal were accusing one another of cheating. In the end, it was Martine Aubry who won – but at what cost? The Socialist Party seemed to be on its uppers.

François decided to walk out through the back door, without trumpeting it in the news. There were no cameras waiting for him. I came to pick him up where he had asked me to meet him. Where no one could see him leave with me…

The next two years were the best years we spent living together. The press said he was unhappy and depressed, they said his political career was over. I did not see the same man they saw. He spent three days a week in Corrèze and the rest of the time we were together. I was in a safe and dull little box at *Paris-Match* – far from political journalism. François wasn't overbooked any more; he no longer had a chauffeur. We lived in our flat on rue Cauchy – he had chosen it himself. We took our time furnishing it, we made time to live, to 'take care of us' as he said. As if nothing else mattered. He would often say: 'We are going to build a nice life for ourselves.'

François made every minute count. The François I

loved passionately at that time was made for happiness. He did not like arguments or sulking between lovers, he disliked anything that could spoil a day, an hour or even a minute. Life was infinitely precious to him.

He was gifted like nobody else at using irony and humour to turn my mood around and put things right. He made me laugh even when I did not want to. He had that amazing quality of seeing only the positive side of things. He devoured life with an uncommon and uplifting optimism.

Back then we would go off on adventures together, listening to our CDs in the car. He could dance the 'sirtaki' to Dalida, even behind the wheel. Just to make me laugh. And laugh I did. I had never laughed so much in my life. Once a week, we would go and lie on the grass somewhere. I took him to places he had never been before. It was with me that he discovered the beauty of the banks of the Loire River – my turf. I made a man who swore only by the Mediterranean and raw sun love the powerful Atlantic tides. He showed me around the villages in his constituency and took me to the Lot region – a place bathed in a golden light.

I remember our first holiday in 2007, an unforgettable holiday in the south of France and in Italy. The following years we holidayed in Spain or Greece. From Athens to Syros, Mykonos and Paros, we behaved like a couple of teenagers, roaming the islands on rental scooters without helmets. We did not know where we would sleep from night to night.

Back then, François still knew how to waste time. We were very close, he could make me laugh over absolutely anything and drove me mad by insisting on driving in the middle of nowhere on a nearly empty petrol tank. I trusted him blindly regardless. He could have taken me anywhere, I would have followed him to the ends of the earth. The only thing that mattered to me was to be with him – wherever he was.

What we shared was unique and unbreakable. Eternal. We could happily spend weeks with only each other for company – there was never a dull moment. He would often repeat: 'I love you because you are a funny lady.' I will admit that later on in our relationship that was not quite so apparent. But I am also certain that he drew a newfound strength from that period which allowed him to overcome the obstacles he later came across.

During that period, I also took François to the *banlieues*, which he did not know well, having won the rural vote. Wearing a cap and sunglasses, he came with me to those discount shops offering a wide range of articles with fast-approaching sell-by dates.

I wanted him to be familiar with the daily lives of some

French citizens who count every single euro and worry about how to make ends meet – every month.

He was the sort of person who would rather not have a meal if it was not first-rate; he did not eat my strawberries unless they were tasty French 'gariguettes'; he did not eat potatoes unless their origin was 'Noirmoutier'; and he wouldn't think twice about binning meat if it had been purchased vacuum-packed. He hardly knew the cost of living. I was always hearing him say 'that's a fair price' for food or articles that were hideously overpriced!

At that time I was making a good living. Even though I incurred heavy costs with the children, I enjoyed a certain financial security. Regardless, I simply could not abide buying something when the price seemed excessive. The difference in our social backgrounds was glaring. He teased me gently, nicknaming me Cosette. He did not understand my hang-up with money. He had never wanted for anything so the notion was completely foreign to him. He wanted the best of everything and only the very best. He enjoyed dining out in fancy restaurants, while I favoured bistros; he was a luxury hotel sort of man, while I was happy with a simple inn.

Not that he was a big spender. In fact he cared very little about his appearance. He would happily buy his shirts and socks in supermarkets. When Ségolène Royal had his luggage couriered to the Socialist Party HQ in June 2007, after their official separation, I sorted through his clothes. I donated most of his clothes to the French charity shop Emmaüs, including the threadbare black velvet suit he loved so much and his leather jackets. I permanently banished his short-sleeved shirts from the wardrobe and we went shopping for a new wardrobe for him.

Three years later, after he had lost nearly two and a half stone in weight, I did the same thing again. I gave away his suits and shirts. He could wear them again today, now that he has put the weight back on, but it is too late: other men – men who shop at Emmaüs – are unknowingly walking around Paris in suits that used to belong to the French President.

Seven years ago, I was going through the luggage Ségolène Royal had filled with his suits. Today it is my turn to box up his things, pack his clothes into suitcases, and have it all delivered to the Élysée Palace... 'Every man for himself / In the bustle of life', as Jeanne Moreau used to sing.

## *May 2014*

When I fell in love with François he was polling at 3 per cent, he was the butt of jokes. Now that he is the

President he is back at 3 per cent, his score when we were at our happiest.

At the moment, in a bid to relive our past, he constantly sends me love messages. He says he needs me. Not an evening goes by without him asking me to have dinner with him. I know he is suffering from the failure of his mandate so far. It is not for want of relentless work, seven days a week. Just like everyone else, I believed in him when he announced with certainty that he would turn around the unemployment rate. I witnessed his disappointment as the months went by and he did not pull it off.

At least at the beginning of his term, François kept his campaign promises. Our only disagreement at the time was the closure of the Florange factory – we had heated arguments about that, each of us fiercely defending our own opinion.

I had not forgotten that intense moment during the campaign when he hauled himself onto the roof of the workers' van and promised he would save their company. I was in favour of the Ministry for Industrial Renewal's proposal to nationalise.

I am no economics expert, but I have eyes and ears. I sensed that voters would be baffled and disappointed by this 180-degree U-turn. When I tried to explain the strength of that symbol and told him that forswearing that promise would be synonymous with impotence and personal betrayal, he simply replied that there was no other option and that was that. There was hardly any point labouring my point any further.

Everything happened so quickly. Today it is an open-and-shut case. The new Economic Adviser at the Élysée comes from a London-based British bank, one of the top City banks. The sound bite in François' former rhetoric, 'finance is my enemy', is long forgotten. His old friend Michel Sapin, the Minister of the Economy, went as far as to say that 'finance is our friend'. Such quiet cynicism! How can voters know what is what? Two years after being elected I sensed that François was lost, and that he had lost his way. 'Change' had certainly happened – but not the change we expected.

I was turning the page and he sensed it. Would he need me as much as this if his popularity ratings had not dropped so drastically?

He writes that he is losing everything and that the last thing that he wants to lose is me.

Five days ago I reminded him of the 'anniversary' of his separation statement. A humiliation I had to withstand four months ago! When it happened, the shock of it numbed me. It was only afterwards that I realised just how traumatising it had been. Once I could see the bigger picture – I had not been aware of the international press coverage. One day, someone told me that they had found out that I had been dismissed from the Élysée on the cover of a Phnom Penh newspaper. Someone else said they had found I had been cheated on in a magazine from Bangkok – or Beijing, or Toronto, and so on and so forth.

I had been thrown to the sharks in international waters without a second thought. I instinctively protected myself but the damage had been done.

Every day in the street, women – for the most part, but there are men too – congratulate me on my 'dignity'. Sometimes I am forced to soften their harsh words against the President. After the first round of the municipal elections, a man came up to me in the street and said: 'I think about you every day. I have always voted for the Socialist Party, but this time I didn't go because of what Hollande did to you.'

My response to him was: 'One can be angry or disappointed, but it's important to vote regardless. I went. In fact, I even voted for the Socialist Party. Because I do not want the National Front to be France's premier party.'

My response seemed to have caught the man off-guard and he looked at me with wide eyes, then nodded his head: 'OK, I'll vote in the second round.'

Another day, young schoolchildren – barely twelve, I'd guess – asked me if I would pose for a picture with them. I said yes, as I always do. One of them said: 'I will never vote for Hollande after what he did to you!' I simply smiled because by the time he comes of voting age, 2017 will have passed already… For these young children, the first vote in presidential election will be in 2022.

Many people share with me their break-up stories and how they were cheated on. They tell me they think I am very strong; sometimes they go as far as describing the change they see in me as a 'metamorphosis'. They say I am less tense, more natural now. I have been freed of the chains of protocol, as I have been freed of the chains of that passion. Day after day, I emerge from the prison without chains or bars of being madly in love.

But the strength people see in me is just a front. I have been medicated for four months. As a prominent psychiatrist put it, 'I have rarely witnessed such a violent shock.' In spite of the treatment, I still occasionally break down over the smallest of things – sometimes all it takes is a minor detail and the brutality of what I went through re-emerges. A fortnight ago, I went to the wedding of a couple of friends. A young lady came to see me and said she was from Tulle: 'You know, in Corrèze, we liked you a lot,' she said. I was unable to control the tears and started sobbing. Hearing about Tulle reminded me of happier times. I was moved to hear that in Corrèze, people appreciated me as I was – they saw beyond the ambitious and manipulative woman I had been painted as.

As days go by, my anger against François grows: how

could he have made such a mess of everything? Our relationship *and* the start of his five-year term. That question keeps going around and around in my head. No doubt in his too. He has written to me to explain himself: 'I was lost and I lost myself.' Not a day goes by without him begging for my forgiveness and asking me to start over. I cannot do it, even if I wanted to. The pain I went through was too strong. As strong as the love I bore him.

Until our separation I was in love with him, wildly so, I would have done anything for him to look at me, to compliment me, to be thoughtful and attentive to me. I was 'crazy in love', as they say. As time went by I was just crazy. His unfaithfulness broke the spell. I loved him too much.

I cannot explain why I failed to see immediately what trap I was falling into. The kiss in Limoges was the starting point of a downward spiral. I cannot understand what prevented me from seeing just how much pain was about to rain down on me. For years, I was out of my depth, blinded and overwhelmed by a love I had long denied. When we said goodbye, early in the morning after our first night together, in Limoges, he came with me to the train station. He did not hide. The night before he had declared his love to me. He did not just want to seduce me, he wanted me to love him. His demands on me kept increasing, and when I in turn said 'I love you', he needed me to love him and no one else, and, eventually, he wanted me to love him more than I had ever loved anyone else before.

Which I did. He had won me over completely. I was under his thumb, he had power over me. He had always managed to get me back, even when I had tried to distance myself, hurt either by something unspoken or by a lie.

Every day he would say that we had lost fifteen years. 'We haven't,' I would reply, 'it was fate.' If our relationship had started fifteen years earlier we might already have separated. As it happens, we did not even last fifteen years…

We had each built a life before and I am proud that my sons look like their father, that they inherited his innate class.

After Limoges, we met in a restaurant we had nicknamed 'the table at the back'. We would have lunch there, hidden away from prying eyes, often until four o'clock. We could never say goodbye. We stayed on the phone for hours. We had so much to say to one another, so much we wanted to share, it was like water finally bursting forth from a dam.

The first summer holidays since our affair had started were fast approaching. I told my husband I had met someone. I did not tell him who it was but he soon found out. Today I understand how distraught he was. Now I know just how far suffering can go, I understand what madness it can elicit.

Just before the summer, François and I were able to steal a few moments of intense happiness. When the time came to go on holiday with our respective families we were beyond miserable. Separating for a month was more than we could bear. I missed everything about him when he was not there. I was under his spell. We spoke of running away together. We eventually gave up on the idea for our children's sake.

He said he was going through hell. But that summer, I saw pictures of him in magazines, looking happy with his family. Was he deceiving me? I never questioned his love. No man had ever shown his love for me as he did.

In September 2005 Ségolène Royal found out about us. She immediately announced that she planned on running in the Socialist Party primaries in an interview with … *Paris-Match*. It was a direct message but François did not take her statement seriously.

The scenario for the latest film noir was being written … The witch-hunt was open and I was the witch. *Paris-Match* had been tipped off by Ségolène Royal and the magazine's board put pressure on me. Moreover, her team threatened me with retribution. Ségolène Royal's supporters also threatened to retaliate. I was worried, but François reassured me, he was certain that things would calm down and that she would not see her primaries candidacy through.

In December, François suggested we move in together. I said no – I was not ready. I feared it would be splashed all over the media. I even had nightmares about it – imagining that I was being exposed naked on a square, that I had nowhere to hide.

The threats were cranked up a notch, and even the *Paris-Match* board was pressured to let me go. François and I tried several times to separate – we each went back to our homes, back to our daily lives. I did not want to be responsible for what would most likely happen: even though he was the First Secretary of the Socialist Party and, accordingly, his party's legitimate candidate, he would not be able to stand in the Socialist Party primaries. Ségolène Royal was defying him in public in hopes that, in private, he would give in. And it was over me that they were duelling…

François did not give in. As it became increasingly apparent that the mother of his children would really stand and that her candidacy was starting to be taken seriously, he continued to tell me that he needed me more than ever. It wasn't because he was stuck. He told me Ségolène Royal had clearly laid out the terms of the bargain: 'If you leave that woman, I will let you stand in the presidential election.'

François had to choose between his political future and me. Once again we tried and failed to separate. Another summer was coming around. We were preparing to go on separate holidays. I was going away alone with my children and François was preparing to play happy families. The perfect family, in fact: the First Secretary of the Socialist Party who was taking a step back for the mother of his children.

Journalists were going mad for this romantic tale, never imagining for a second that it was turning into a nightmare. The media monster had been created and needed feeding.

Meanwhile, Ségolène Royal's anger and suffering over the problems in her relationship – which she kept quiet about – fuelled her ambition and energy. She had become unstoppable. There were more and more polls in her favour. She was leading in the race. François asked all his friends to support her and denied it to my face. He knew he was out of the game; she had won. All things considered, he preferred Ségolène Royal to win over Dominique Strauss-Kahn, Laurent Fabius or Lionel Jospin – who had attempted a political comeback in the summer of 2006.

I very nearly went to see the former Prime Minister to tell him the truth of the matter. I considered explaining that François was tied down by a personal dilemma and could therefore not publicly announce his ambition to run in the Socialist primaries. In the end I decided against it: I was a journalist, it was not my place, and I would have felt like I was betraying François.

Ségolène Royal was appointed with flying colours. I was stunned. I wanted to put an end to my relationship with François as I had no wish to participate in the media lie of a united couple backing one another in the Élysée race – the French version of Bill and Hillary Clinton. I did not want to be an accomplice to this farce. I felt like I was in a bad film that could only end in disaster.

The who's who of politics and media in Paris had heard about our affair. *Paris-Match* editorial meetings had become hell. When the subject of the Hollande–Royal couple came up, all eyes were on me. I did not look away, but I paid the price for it.

The last straw was another lie from François, one too many. My mind was made up, this time I really was going to leave him. I did, and stayed silent for three weeks – I was gritting my teeth. A friend in common told me that François had never been so unhappy but was determined to stay strong for once … until one Sunday morning he stopped me on my way to the market. He had been waiting for me for hours.

He got me back – yet again. I didn't know whether to laugh or to cry. His strength of persuasion was nuclear.

Despite his love for me, he campaigned for Ségolène

Royal after she won in the primaries. For her, he went on the electoral trail all over France with barely any media coverage – conversely, 'the candidate', as he called her, was idolised in meetings. He gave her campaign his all, I can bear witness to that. He put so much energy and time into campaigning for her that we saw each other very infrequently. He wanted his side to win but, from January 2007, he was increasingly doubtful about Ségolène Royal's chances.

Royal's credibility was dropping, polls reflected voters' doubts. François must have told me a million times that she wasn't up to the task. There is a world of difference between a traditional political career and running for the Élysée. You need to be on top of economic and geopolitical subjects – a mass of knowledge and relations you cannot acquire in just a few weeks.

People started to talk about the in-fighting – the party and the campaign team had strong differences of opinion, mirroring the disagreements between Ségolène Royal and François Hollande. The two of them had practically no direct contact. She had set up camp in her campaign HQ. Often it was through AFP news items that François found out about new promises Ségolène Royal had made, and he always saw the latest party posters after everyone else.

On the one hand we were going through a nightmare in public; on the other we were living a private dream.

The idea of being together after the election was what kept us going. Deep down, I was convinced that if she was elected he would not leave her. Despite his promises, I did not believe him.

We managed to spend a night together in the midst of all this and the next morning we switched the radio on to listen to the news in bed. The first round of the presidential election was only a month away and the topic was Ségolène Royal's upcoming campaign book. In it she wrote, 'Yes, we are together: yes, François and I still live together' and went on to outline her plans of marrying him on a canoe in Tahiti. François was furious, he felt trapped.

For all that, on the evening of the first round when it became apparent that Nicolas Sarkozy had secured victory, François was despondent. The rest is history. A few weeks after Ségolène Royal's defeat, in a piece on Royal's campaign entitled 'The femme fatale', two *Le Monde* journalists revealed that Hollande was in a relationship with an unnamed woman, and sparked off an explosion.

Ségolène Royal wasted no time announcing in turn that she had 'asked François Hollande to leave the family home'. The AFP rushed to make her sentence an 'urgent' news report, even though the former couple had agreed on a joint statement.

All is fair in love and war and I now fully appreciate

how betrayal can lead to so much resentment. I can easily imagine that during that period François behaved with Ségolène Royal as he did with me during his affair with Julie Gayet – which is to say that he was the king of doublespeak, ambiguity and perpetual lies.

At the time, we lived in a small furnished flat that I loved but François did not want to stay there. He wanted us to move in together properly. We chose the flat I am still in, on rue Cauchy, and spent time furnishing it to our liking.

I caught wind of a rumour about him regretting his separation and wanting to get back with Ségolène Royal. She certainly suggested as much. Meanwhile, he was more committed than ever, and was very insistent about wanting me to bear his child.

Anything is possible, including that Ségolène Royal was telling the truth … I now know how duplicitous François Hollande can be.

François missed his children. He had not seen them in months and they collectively refused to see him as long as he stayed with me. I did not want to be responsible for this estrangement.

Nothing is more important in my eyes than children. I have shared custody of my three boys and I miss them half of the week.

So I told François that I was willing to try for a baby with him, but only once he had rekindled his relationship with his children. François did reconcile with his children but nature did not give us the child he had been dreaming of since we met. It is probably for the best.

Not long ago, I read a book about François Hollande in which he told the author that he had never wanted a child with me. I was mortified. He then justified himself to me by saying: 'I wasn't about to share our intimacy.'

One more lie, and possibly the most hurtful he could ever have uttered.

## June 2014

I can't switch the radio on without hearing about the commemoration of the Allied landings in Normandy on 6 June. When I was at the Élysée, my team and I discussed a First Lady D-Day tribute. We had planned to visit a factory which had continued to operate during the war thanks to women – while their husbands, brothers and sons were fighting in the war.

Now, hearing about the D-Day commemorations is like reliving the whole January nightmare all over again. I feel myself sinking into a bottomless sadness – the sort you don't easily snap out of. The past keeps engulfing me, stifling me like an adder curling itself around my neck.

Every afternoon I end up back in my bed, unable to read or write. I cannot do anything. Anything at all. I simply cannot let go and move forward.

When I do go out, no one notices a thing. People even say I am 'radiant'. But I am unable to project myself professionally, my plans are very vague.

Today, Friday, I cannot see how to get through the day – short of staying in bed with a couple of sleeping pills for company. As they often have, my friends are the ones who end up saving me from this dark day that reminds me so much of the past.

As if to rub salt into my wounds, François continues to harass me with text messages. The day before yesterday he swore he thought only of me. Yesterday, he begged me to see him again. This morning, he said he wanted me back, no matter what price he would have to pay. Sometimes he sends me a dozen texts a day. Short and haunting sentences about missing me, about making amends, about how much he needs us to resume our former life. He seems tired of losing everything, both in his personal and his public life.

When he does not have a reception or an official dinner, he asks me to have dinner with him. He tries to keep track of my evenings out and my trips. In New York or in Marrakech, I find flowers waiting for me in my hotel room – even though I never tell him where I am staying.

He has stepped up symbolic gestures and impassioned declarations of love.

But he continues to lie to me, to make promises he does not keep. Getting back together is a doomed prospect because I know he will not change. While he is begging me to come back, he is also turning the 'Madame wing' into an office for his advisers – whose numbers are forever growing. As I write, there is no one in my former office. It is only a matter of time.

He swears he is prepared to issue a public apology. I do not believe him. I no longer believe any of his promises. Every single one of his lies has eaten away at the boundless love we bore one another.

Early June 2014 is a difficult time for me – everything seems to happen all at once, as is often the case.

First, the start of the celebrations to commemorate D-Day. As I had feared, I find that I am simply unable to listen to any information about the 70th anniversary of that historical day, much less watch footage. So on the eve of the anniversary of the Normandy landings, I watch an interview Putin is giving on French television. Disgusted with his phallocratic statements, I tweet: 'Glad not to have to shake Putin's hand'. Whether his comments were lost in translation essentially makes very little difference as my tweet related more broadly to his enterprise and everything he stands for as an individual in power:

racism, homophobia, depriving people of freedoms, wanting to carve out a chunk of Ukraine… My tweet receives a mixed response, some support me and some insult me. It is the same old song: 'In what capacity are you speaking out? You are nothing but the President's cuckold.' I don't know what I should answer. I express my views just like the seven million other people who use that social network in France – people are free to ignore me.

There is more in store for me: I hear that *Closer* is running a front-page story announcing that François is still seeing Julie Gayet in secret. He immediately sends me a text message swearing that it is a complete fabrication. It feels like déjà-vu, back to several months ago when he was fiercely denying the persistent rumour – called it 'hogwash', in fact.

He assures me that this time he isn't lying, says he has no reason to do so. I scroll through my phone and find his loving message from yesterday – he promises he will go with me wherever I go, that we will live together again. The whole business is insane now, it has become window-dressing – smoke and mirrors – and it is completely impossible to separate the lies from the truth.

François over-exerts himself … Between dining with Barack Obama and another dinner with Vladimir Putin, he has found the time to text me again to deny the news that has emerged and assure me that I am the love of his life. He compartmentalises different areas of his life and somehow piles them all on top of each other – time is elastic for him. The President is trying to rekindle our romance, which keeps dying one more death – and all the while he is dealing with the most sensitive world affairs, on the eve of an historic commemoration. He is a politician through and through: he can lead several parallel lives, be active on all fronts at once.

At the end of the day, whether he is lying to me or not, does it really make a difference to me? I have decided to turn over a new leaf. This sudden new development helps me do that: it convinces me that François will never change, that lying is a deep-rooted part of him, part and parcel of his personality. 'Powerful men soon lose any sense of limits,' the psychiatrist who treated me after I went to hospital explained. They call it 'winners' syndrome'.

I WITNESSED THE change in that man. In 2010, when we arrived at the Socialist Party's summer conference in La Rochelle, he had lost a lot of weight. I encouraged him, I helped him, but I never forced him to lose weight. We were both fit and healthy. We had taken a month and a half holiday. I tried to prepare him for the way the press would react and how the physical change would be interpreted. He did not believe any of it. He could not believe that anyone might assume he was planning to run based on that fact that he was nearly two stone lighter on the scales. But that was precisely how all the journalists and many Socialist voters interpreted the physical change in him — as evidence of determination. People started saying that François Hollande was preparing to run for President.

That September he was the star, everyone was talking about him. After five years of disgrace, five years in the political wilderness, it looked like he might get his chance to shine. At the time, people said I had a positive influence on him.

Those favourable comments did not last. His new look, his changed taste in ties and the fact that he had lost the short-sleeved shirts were one thing – I could be credited for all of that – but his macho entourage would not hear of any involvement on my part politically speaking, even though I had worked as a political journalist for eighteen years. So I rarely took part in meetings with his 'friends'.

François nevertheless insisted that I attend an important meeting, early 2011, to decide how he would announce his candidacy. There couldn't have been more than ten participants at the meeting – and I was the only woman – the idea being to guarantee confidentiality. Four of his closest political allies and friends were there, as well as two PR specialists. I felt like a wallflower among them. Until they unveiled their plan: an interview in the regional daily press. I couldn't get over how unoriginal it was. I reminded them that Jacques Chirac had made his announcement in November 1994 in the exact same way.

'But the idea is to reduce the risks as much as possible,' one of them objected.

I insisted: 'Might as well not run if it's about not taking any risks.'

I think that from that day onward they had a problem with me. I had dared defy that group of proud peacocks who dreamt of power but were hardly ready for it. François had originally wanted to make a formal statement from his fiefdom in Tulle and I was convinced that it was a far better idea. The debate continued, but no decision was taken. When the meeting was over, François asked me what my take on it was: 'The best solution is the one that feels most natural to you. You will shine, I don't doubt it for a second.'

He went for the Tulle option.

But he had a long and lonely road ahead of him. No one took his candidacy in the Socialist primaries seriously. François had announced that the condition for him to run was that he be elected head of the Corrèze

General Council. Everyone saw it as a fake challenge but there was a real risk involved. In the event, he overcame that first hurdle.

He and I agreed that I would not be there on the day he announced his candidacy – 31 March 2011. He did not want the image of a couple going on the campaign trail together. As for me, I was still doing my political show, *Campaign Profiles*, on television, which made campaigning with him a potential conflict of interest. It was one of the worst frustrations of my life, it was absolute torture not to be there.

I planned to watch him live on my computer, locked up alone in my *Paris-Match* office. I might even have missed it, had a colleague not warned me that the time had been changed. None of the members of François' team had passed on the information. François had already begun his speech when I caught it.

'I cannot accept the state France is in, I will not let France give in to pessimism … I cannot bear the suffering which too many French citizens experience.'

His tone was firm and convincing throughout his eight minutes and seventeen seconds.

'I will put France first,' he said, with a newfound assurance. 'I have decided to present my candidacy in the presidential election by running in the Socialist primary elections.'

The crowd cheered and called out 'François for President'.

I burst into tears of emotion mingled with unspeakable frustration. How I wished I could have been by his side! I waited for his call, as nervous and excited as a young girl.

He did call but it was a very short call – he was about to climb into his car with a journalist and head back to Paris. No time for banter. I waited for him for dinner as we had planned to go to the restaurant to celebrate. When he arrived, another disappointment was in store for me: his team had planned to send him to Boulogne-sur-Mer, if I remember correctly, so he could be with the fishermen at sunrise. He only had half an hour to spare. Again, it hadn't occurred to anyone – not even him – to let me know.

I called his campaign manager and we had a heated exchange. He said that from now on if I wished to spend an evening with François, I would have to run it by him. That was unthinkable. I agreed to the idea of a campaign and I was willing to concede that our personal life would never be the same. But asking someone for an appointment in order to see François was out of the question. François' campaign manager would not budge, and neither would I, because we both knew that the lost ground would never be recovered.

In the end, François settled the matter with a compromise

– something he is very good at. He and I had a romantic dinner together and then he got on the road. The die was cast: we would all have to live in constant uncertainty – we would be dependent on François' whims, his decisions or lack thereof.

I felt a sense of loss grow in me from that moment. In the primaries campaign I can't say I was written out of the script altogether, but it did feel like I had been given a role without any lines. Much like in a silent film noir, no one spoke to me: I was not kept informed of what was going on. Nor did I play a very active role: for the sake of remaining discreet, I did not go on trips with François.

I only attended the very first meeting in Clichy. I sat at the back of the room, as if I was a stranger. So much so, in fact, that I was thrown out after the meeting because the theatre was closing and had to wait for François in my car for an hour and a half. François was in a room next door, with his favourite companions: the journalists. He did not bother to let me know. His candidacy absorbed all of his attention and I was blending into the background.

AS FOR HIS entourage, their reactions to me varied. Many of them came to tell me that François was a changed man thanks to me; conversely, his old guard elephants kept me at arm's length. It was out of the question that I should steal 'their François'. Knives were out. Typical. But what did they want? What did they think? We were not playing the same game. Obviously not. It was all very childish.

Many doubted that François' candidacy had any future. When the preliminary meetings of the 'Hollandaise' political club – called Répondre à gauche[14] – were held, there were more than a few empty seats. I was always there, in the back row. He pretended we did not know each other. I put it down to a sense of propriety.

He outlined his campaign themes, which focused on youth – but his audience was very small – there were hardly even any journalists.

His popularity ratings were not taking off. He remained stoic and showed no signs of discouragement, even in front of me. His dogged determination was inspiring. Meanwhile, for the press, 'real' campaigning only started when Dominique Strauss-Kahn got into the race. That was when the press started taking notice. Everyone who was anyone in politics and media wanted to know whether François would stay the course. No matter how many times I repeated that he would, no one believed me. I for one was absolutely convinced of it. He was

---

14 A Socialist Response.

single-minded like never before. He felt certain he would beat Dominique Strauss-Kahn. He sensed that the people wanted stronger Socialist ideas, that it was important to position himself in opposition to the Sarkozy persona, his outrageous excesses, his fascination with money, his transgressions. In François' mind, Dominique Strauss-Kahn and Nicolas Sarkozy were similar animals.

A secret rendezvous was organised between him and Dominique Strauss-Kahn, at his home, opposite the restaurant La Closerie des Lilas. I dropped François off in my car and went to wait for him at the bar. 'The American' wanted to sound out 'the Man from Corrèze'.

François later told me that he confirmed to him he would not pull out. Dominique Strauss-Kahn did not interpret their meeting in the same way. It was impossible to know who was telling the truth as there were only two players in their game of Liar's Dice.

On 15 May 2011, as we often did on weekends when the weather was nice, we went to my house in L'Isle-Adam. François enjoyed gardening and going to the market on Sunday – afterwards we would do justice to Jean-Jacques' meat – my favourite butcher.

That Saturday, we went to bed a little before midnight. I always keep my mobile near, just like every other worried mother when her children are out.

Around 1 a.m., just as I was starting to nod off, my

phone started to vibrate. A friend who was at the Cannes Film Festival – which I was heading to the following day for my show – had sent me a few text messages to let me know that Dominique Strauss-Kahn had been arrested.

I decided to wake François and tell him what was going on. 'Go back to sleep, it's a crock of shit,' he said with his back turned to me. He had never heeded the rumours about his rival's sexual deviance. It is one of François' qualities: he ignores malicious talk around town. François fell back asleep. I was wide awake: I browsed the internet, searching for more reliable sources in respected US newspapers.

I woke François up again a few hours later, it must have been around two or three in the morning. 'Trust me, something serious is happening,' I said, 'the US press has announced that Dominique Strauss-Kahn has been arrested for rape.'

This time, François sat up immediately, propped himself against his pillow and he too started looking at his iPhone. He did not waste a minute mocking Dominique Strauss-Kahn. Mentally, François was already preparing his next move: 'It's bad news, now Socialists are likely to rally around his other Socialist rival, Martine Aubry.'

Our phones started ringing off the hook, we received calls from his entourage and from journalists clamouring for statements. We barely slept a wink all night. The rest is history. The media craze that followed, a worldwide snowball effect with thousands of journalists, genuine and fake researchers, backed by hundreds of commentators with more than a bit of nerve, all trying to outdo each other with new 'information'. Experts came out of the woodwork, there were endless hours of live feed showing the non-stop parade of cars with tinted windows and twenty-second events on a loop, while dozens of rumours – no fact-checking there! – were sucked in and spat out by the media monster.

It never occurred to me that I too would one day be the object of such insanity.

François was completely thrown. He had built his entire campaign around his opposition with Dominique Strauss-Kahn. Consequently, he needed to rethink it entirely. As he had feared, some Socialists started asking for the primaries to be cancelled and for the Socialist First Secretary, Martine Aubry, to be automatically nominated sole candidate.

The very first person to step forward in support of Martine Aubry was an elected representative from a Parisian *banlieue*. A few days earlier he had come over for dinner with his wife and said he would support Dominique Strauss-Kahn except if the latter stood down, in which case he would choose François – on no account would he vote for Martine Aubry, he said.

Over dinner he heavily criticised Martine Aubry, calling her 'crazy and unstable' and attacking her over her behaviour in private matters. François was quite clearly his second choice but he was outspoken and I liked that. His public support for Martine Aubry only a few days after attacking her in private was a major political backflip. A betrayal of such magnitude – pulled off with disconcerting ease – was beyond me and I texted him to tell him what I thought of him. Sadly, that is just one example of human behaviour in the hornets' nest that is politics.

Late June 2011, when Ségolène Royal started campaigning for the Socialist Party primaries, things got a bit more complicated ... Until the very last minute, François was convinced she would pull out. He was wrong.

The clash between the two 'exes' was Christmas come early for the press. The primaries looked set to turn into a face-off like no other before it. All the ingredients were there – getting even for 2007, the defeat and the separation. Ségolène Royal was merciless, asking, on national television: 'Can you list a single one of François Hollande's achievements in thirty years in politics?'

She was spoiling for a fight but François never counterattacked. He knew all too well that public opinion would not take kindly to a frontal attack. Besides, there were the children to think of. The whole episode was no doubt painful for them but when they came for lunch or dinner at our flat on rue Cauchy, the subject was never touched upon. At least not when I was around.

After the first round, François Hollande and Martine Aubry were the only two candidates still standing. I heard on the radio, in my car, that François had reached an agreement with Ségolène Royal: she would support him in his campaign and encourage her followers to vote for François. I was so shocked I hit the brakes abruptly and nearly had an accident. François had not breathed a word to me.

I sensed that, as usual, he was unable to discuss even the simplest things directly. I knew what Ségolène Royal had asked for in exchange for her rallying – and not just financially. I never doubted for a minute that she had obtained what she wanted.

I tweeted to congratulate her on her 'sincere and disinterested rallying'. Only a small number of people in my inner circle understood the sarcasm. At the time, in a bid to defuse the situation, I put up with and even disregarded François' omissions and secretiveness. Now that I know the pervasive effects of lies, I cannot abide them any longer.

I followed François throughout his campaign the way you hold on to – or are dragged along by – the man you love. I went along with him on the way to his dream.

He did not reciprocate. With the Socialist primaries in full swing, in September 2011 I gave up my political show and changed course. I was still working for the same channel but I was now interviewing artists – singers, actors, and so on – for a show called *Itinéraires*.[15] One day when I mentioned my show, François turned around and asked: 'What's *Itinéraires*?' I was astounded, the man I was sharing my life with did not even know the name of the show I was presenting. Nothing I did interested him.

That he had never watched a single episode of my TV show should not have come as a surprise, as he did not read my book reviews for *Paris-Match* either. I would see him skip the culture section to get to the politics pages.

There had been a time when I was so important in his eyes, when I was a political journalist. It was long gone.

Outside of politics, François was interested in nothing. Nothing and no one. He was not interested in literature and was just as indifferent to theatre and music. Cinema interested him somewhat – just maybe. His circle of friends never extended beyond the so-called 'Voltaire' year at the elite École nationale d'administration. Not politics? Not interested.

---

15  *Itineraries.*

No one was more valuable to François than a political journalist. I was often asked whether journalists were jealous of me and I would reply that no, it was quite the opposite: I was the one who was jealous of them. Envious of his closeness to them, the fascination he had for them. There were often journalists at home – they dropped by to give the Socialist candidate some advice.

In spite of everything, I stubbornly continued to love him and only him. The summer break after he announced he would run was anything but. François did not want to leave France and planned to campaign during that time. He met us in Hossegor, where I had rented a house for the summer to spend the holidays with my children. When they went to spend the rest of the holiday with their father, François and I roamed the inside of the French Basque Country, which I did not know very well. We found a lovely little inn, my perfect holiday. For François, each stop was an opportunity to meet the elected representatives, to try to rally them around. That was how we found ourselves at a pastorale – four hours of Basque songs, outdoors in 14 degrees Celsius … in August. It proved useful, as the Senator rallied! Every vote counted and I knew that.

François was spinning his web. Patiently. We went to Latche together, François Mitterrand's den. His son

Gilbert Mitterrand did the honours. Danielle Mitterrand was there, weak but happy, surrounded by her grand-daughters and her great-grandsons. She welcomed us with open arms. Neither François nor I had ever visited François Mitterrand's property. Discovering this place – the sheep pen François Mitterrand liked to retire to, surrounded by his books – was incredibly emotional!

Nothing had changed since then. Not even his collection of paperbacks. This was a historic place – where François Mitterrand had seen several heads of state. Gilbert insisted on keeping the place just as it was, with its dust – as if time had stopped. The donkeys still had the same names, Noisette[16] and Marron.[17] Like their owner, the animals were not immortal and had been replaced since François Mitterrand's death. The trees were 'his trees' – the trees Mitterrand used to speak to. Their roots run deep, just as Mitterrand will always remain deep-rooted in history. I was keenly aware of the privilege it was to be there – I sensed I was embarking upon an extraordinary adventure.

The day after his victory against Martine Aubry, François was happier than ever. We had had a short night's sleep and stayed in bed awhile, listening to the radio.

---

16  Hazel.

17  Chestnut.

The news bulletins all opened with François' appointment as the Socialist Party's officially endorsed candidate. François' face radiated intense happiness. I still have that picture saved on my iPhone… A picture of ecstatic joy and fulfilment. An expression I had never since seen on him.

From the very start, I had been convinced that if he won the Socialist primaries, he would win the presidential election. I had no doubt about that, and I do not think he did either.

He remained in a state of extreme concentration and complete self-control throughout the entire official campaign. Being the favourite contender entailed a risk: the slightest faux pas could cost him dear. The week before the big Le Bourget meeting, the defining moment of his campaign, François did not leave the rue Cauchy for three days.

Aquilino Morelle, his PR adviser, the man whose shoes were always shined, claimed to have authored the Le Bourget speech.[18] In truth, François worked very hard at it. The dining room table was covered in notes and the floor was strewn with pages and pages of drafts. I took

---

18 A public scandal had arisen following accusations of Morelle leading an inappropriately lavish lifestyle, including hiring a personal shoe-shiner to clean his many pairs of handmade leather shoes.

refuge in our room so as not to disturb him but every so often he would come and find me to ask me to print out new notes he was receiving by email because he didn't know how to do it himself. I was his little helper.

I listened to the radio on the hour, every hour. I became aware that expectations were building around his speech. Commentators expected him to open up to the French public for the first time and give some personal details. A presidential election is a meeting between a man and a people. In the evening, I asked him if he would let me read his speech. He gave it to me and I found nothing personal in it, nothing about him, about his background. I waited until we were in bed with the lights out to tell him what I thought of his speech: 'Why not say something personal, talk about what you owe your parents? Why not say you love people? That's what's expected of you. You are going to disappoint everyone if you don't. You simply can't hold anything back.'

François barely answered but I heard him get up to work on his speech. The next day, he showed me his new draft. It was better, but it still fell short. Again, I challenged him to dig deeper, and he did. He gave it his all. I felt like I had helped him bring his own thoughts to life. A few extra paragraphs were all it took, but those paragraphs would make all the difference to the journalists.

Jamel Bensalah directed the campaign film that would
be shown to the Socialist supporters at the all-important
Le Bourget meeting. He wanted to show it to us beforehand but François did not want to hear or see anything,
he wanted to focus on his speech. I asked Jamel to wait
for me outside our flat and went to watch the film with
him in his car. It was very well directed, it was pacy
and carried the energy and spirit of the campaign. But
I immediately identified a problem: 'Jamel, this won't
work. There is no footage of Ségolène Royal! And the
blame is going to be laid on me.'

'It has nothing to do with either you or her. It is not
an archive documentary. It was a deliberate decision on
my part, as director, to only show victories.'

'They are all going to attack me with fists flying.'

I was insistent, but he refused to believe me. He did
not realise that the media monster was already on the
rampage: every single word and fact was ripped apart
and dissected, over-analysed and over-interpreted – seen
through the filter of our history.

I was right. The Le Bourget meeting was a huge success, François shone, he was impressive – the blunder
the director had made was the one fly in the ointment.

Though we have certainly had our differences, I can
easily imagine how wounding it was for Ségolène Royal
– a proud politician, the first woman to run for President

in France, and to be a runner-up – when, surrounded by tens of thousands of ecstatic Socialist Party members, she discovered that the film did not have a single image of her campaign.

Her entourage and the press unanimously laid the blame for her conspicuous absence at my door. Jamel Bensalah immediately sent me a huge bouquet of flowers to apologise, but his mea culpa did not stand a chance against the media's version.

The incident helped make the Hollande/Royal saga popular all over again. At the beginning of his campaign, François had given me his word that he would never hold a joint meeting with Ségolène Royal – just group meetings with other Socialist leaders. Unsurprisingly, under media and political pressure, a public meeting was nonetheless organised in Rennes, between the two successive Socialist Party presidential candidates.

Cue several trying hours of collective hysteria – in which I participated. I literally felt – which is to say I was the dictionary definition of the term – 'uncontrollable emotional excesses'. I was physically incapable of watching them both hand in hand on stage – especially as that gesture was exactly what everyone wanted: the party members just as much as the media. I was powerless in the face of the collective desire to see them side by side.

I had barely arrived when a journalist, with a cameraman

in tow, called out to me: 'How does it make you feel to see François Hollande rebuilding his relationship?'

He did not bother with common decency. His question was delivered like you do an uppercut: it is direct and you aim where it hurts.

I said nothing. I simply turned my back to him. But I was with another journalist and he *did* put his shock into words: '*Now* I understand what you have to put up with.' I still remember how aghast he looked. As for me, on the outside I wore a mask, but a fire was raging on the inside.

Seeing my state of nervous tension, François' team suggested I walk through the huge auditorium alongside him. The idea was simply preposterous and I refused to do it. I locked myself up in the dressing room waiting for Ségolène Royal to finish her speech and hand over the baton to François.

That morning, François had guaranteed to me that they would not be together on stage, that they would behave like politicians, not like a celebrity couple… We had a tense exchange in the dressing room. Things got a bit out of hand. I knew Ségolène Royal's personality well enough to guess what would happen next. Contrary to what had been agreed, she obviously went back on stage to be cheered with him. It was so predictable! She could simply not resist such a perfect opportunity to share the spotlight and reassert her pre-eminence. I hit rock bottom, convinced that François and I would never be seen as a bona fide couple.

But just when I thought I was defeated, an idea came to me. At the Le Bourget meeting, I had tried to greet Ségolène Royal, but she turned away as soon as she saw me walk towards her. I had not pushed it, as it was crystal clear that she would refuse to shake my hand there and then. So I decided to give her no choice about it. I waited for her to return to her seat, then I signalled to a few photographers to follow me and made a bee-line to where she was sitting. I tricked her ... Royal style! She had no other option than to shake my hand. I know it was childish of me but it gave me satisfaction to know that our picture, too, would endure.

None of this puts anyone in a flattering light – starting with me. I do not like to lose control of my emotions. I hated feeling like a bundle of nerves, I had my heart in my mouth – perhaps quite literally so. The incident was evidence – if any further evidence was needed – of just how much François' constant doublespeak affected me. Clearly, he did not know how to handle the tensions between me and the mother of his children. I had neither the resources nor the self-confidence to rise above it and François certainly did nothing to reassure me.

I understood that the whole affair had been so heavily publicised and commented on in the media that we were condemned to live on tenterhooks, never able to relax. Widespread media presence and the 'connectedness' of our brave new world – where every single act and gesture is subjected to comments and can create a buzz – make it 'difficult to handle private affairs in private'. I use the expression most deliberately here, as I am the one who coined it, following the 'infamous tweet'…

On the eve of 14 July 2012 – his first television appearance as the new French President – François was busy working on his answers to questions journalists were likely to ask. He was at a loss to turn the 'infamous' page. I prompted him: 'Private affairs should be handled in private'. The next day, François hit a bull's eye with the sound bite. Journalists interpreted it as a scathing condemnation of my behaviour, never imagining that I had inflicted this public censure upon myself…

Right after his television appearance, which itself followed the Champs-Élysées parade, I went with the President on a trip to Brest. François spent his time avoiding me or running off without waiting for me – except for a brief moment to allow photographers to get a few shots of us together, but not alone. I tried to follow him, like his dog – I had not yet realised I was soon to become 'his dog's shadow' on a very short leash. Still, I put a brave smile on and even tried to joke with the journalists: 'From now on, I will bite my thumb before I tweet!'

The journalists appreciated my bon mot. François did not.

Was it because of the tweet rift, the ego of a brand new President or that 'winners' syndrome' which leaders who have made it to a position of power are at risk of, and which, when it hits, makes them lose all sense of empathy? Whatever the case, in the weeks following his election I witnessed a drastic reversal in his feelings for me. He blamed me for anything and everything. That I was an easy target for the media made no difference: he did not have a kind word for me, he neither comforted nor supported me. Even worse, he shot me down.

Six months later, for the first time, a favourable article came out, in *Le Monde*, on the day of the children's Christmas at the Élysée, mid-December. When François read it, he flew into a rage against me, I had never seen him take his anger out on me so violently and I could not understand what had brought this on. I burst into tears. I eventually understood that *Le Monde* was 'his' newspaper – that it should only mention him, and I should make myself scarce. The time when we loved each other and were happy was long gone. Deep down, François wanted me to take a step back, to be invisible. But he did not say it in so many words – his anger was never about what it was purportedly about, to my bewilderment.

As a result of his refusal to address his dissatisfaction

with me head-on, his behaviour became boorish. Just before a state dinner, after complimenting me on my outfit, he suddenly asked: 'Does it take you a long time to be so beautiful?'

'A bit of time, yes,' I replied.

'Then again, it's not like you have anything better to do.' I thought he was joking, but he was not. He stared at me, cold and unsmiling. In his mind, I was there to make him look good but I was no good to him. And there I was, dressed up to the nines – I had tried to look pretty for him, so he would be proud of me. On another occasion, he barked: 'Go get changed! Get dressed!' because he thought my dress was too sexy. He wanted to bring me to heel and I had to stand up for myself: I agreed to wear a wrap over my bare shoulders, but that was where I drew the line.

Slowly but surely, his cutting remarks made me lose every last scrap of self-confidence. One day I mentioned that I had bumped into Cécilia Sarkozy at the Unitaid dinner, and that in front of Bill Clinton she had said: 'Without you, Hollande would never have been elected.' I know how instrumental she was in Nicolas Sarkozy's career and I admired her courage when she walked out. François froze.

His reply was scathing: 'If it makes you happy to believe that you had something to do with it…'

I kept my cool: 'Some people think so, at any rate, even though it embarrasses you.'

I felt very lost having to justify my existence in his life. Did our love still mean anything to him?

*2014...*

I went to bed very late last night. I cannot get out of bed now. Nor can I go back to sleep. This has happened a lot since our separation. I switch the radio on and it half sends me to sleep. Suddenly, a radio show on *France Inter* catches my attention. It is called *Service Public*[19] on upwards social mobility – the theme being 'It is *not* written'.

A memoirist talks about his childhood in social services, and then going home to live with his alcoholic mother and stepfather. He is now CEO of an SME. A researcher on the show said something which really hit home for me: 'When you climb the social ladder, you have to remember to stay true to yourself, and you often hurt for other people.'

Why is it only when other people explain self-evident things that I finally understand them? I have 'gone up in

---

19 *Public Service.*

the world' since my days in the *banlieue* in Angers, but I am not myself anymore and I am a ball of hurt, everything hurts, and I hurt for other people. That old feeling of not being legitimate haunts me throughout the duration of the radio show. Is vertical mobility the reason why I always felt illegitimate – both in my relationship and at the Elysée Palace? Why was I so in love with a man whom I had nothing in common with?

I remember a Christmas dinner one evening at my mother's in Angers, with my brothers and sisters, their spouses, and my nephews and nieces – all twenty-five of us.

After dinner, François turned to me and said with a snicker: 'Well, the Massonneaus certainly ain't a pretty bunch…'

It was like a slap in the face and still stings, months later. How could François have said that about my family? So the Massonneau family is 'not a pretty bunch', is it? Well, it certainly is typical of the people who voted for him.

Though it is very revealing of who François is, I was reluctant to tell that anecdote because it is hurtful for my family, who were so happy to get to know him and so proud to have him for dinner.

But I want to wash away so many lies, emerge from this book without the burden of so many unspoken things.

I want to apologise to you, my family, for having fallen in love with a man who could snigger about the Massonneaus not being 'a pretty bunch'. I am proud of you. Not one of my brothers and sisters has gone astray. Some have made it, some less so, but we all know how to reach out and express our love for each other. The words 'family' and 'solidarity' really mean something – for François they are purely abstract. Not once has he invited his father or his brother to the Élysée Palace. He wants to single himself out – a President who is proudly alone.

Which side of the tracks do you have to be born on to look like 'a pretty bunch'? Granted, in my family, no one has been to a 'Grandes école' – not for us, the École nationale d'administration or the equally prestigious école des Hautes Études Commerciales, known as HEC. None of us owns a clinic, none of us have done business in real estate like his father. None of us owns a property in Mougins on the French Riviera – unlike François. None of us are senior civil servants, none of us are famous – like the people he has been socialising with since the 'Voltaire year' of the École Nationale d'administration. The Massonneaus are a French working-class family. Working class but proud of who we are.

His sentence was so full of bile and spite, it haunts me and now that the spell is broken, I am freed from the magic of the way he looked at me. He made himself out to be the man who doesn't like rich people but in truth the President doesn't like the poor. This Socialist privately calls them 'the toothless', proud of his quip.

I thought back with bitterness to my family who 'ain't a pretty bunch' when I found out that during his affair with Julie Gayet, François had been to her parents' lavish château – seventeenth-century walls surrounded by a magnificent park. It is certainly more stylish than a council flat in a small-town *banlieue*! Much nicer than a mobile home in the middle of a starless campsite not too far from the sea.

Now there's a family just as François likes them: a surgeon for a grandfather, an antique dealer for a grandmother, a renowned doctor and adviser to ministers for a father. A tidy little world, a 'pretty' little world, a 'boho' little world, with its fine and refined taste, where the guests are famous, where everyone votes Socialist but no one knows how much minimum wage is. Back home we don't need notes drafted by ministerial advisers to know that. You just have to look at the bottom of your payslip.

People have called me a *bourgeoise*, cold and cruel – I was simply not in my own world. Illegitimate, and doubly so. After the separation statement, my family stood behind me. You don't get forsaken in the Massonneau family. They all stood and supported me. That man who played nice guy, telling jokes at the dinner table, was bored with that 'not-a-pretty-sight' family and favoured dinners in town.

A shame: he could have learned a lot from the Masson-neau family about the way the French feel: we don't beat around the bush, we don't lie, we call a spade a spade, we tell it like it is and we look people in the eyes when we do.

KING OF EQUIVOCAL remarks, François also said to me one day: 'What I love about you is that you never forget where you are from.'

How could I? Rumour has it that I have inherited colossal wealth from my banker grandfather who died before my birth – as if France had never seen a single family climb down the social ladder.

Would my mother have worked as a cashier if we had had that kind of money? A five-year-old would figure out that it makes no sense, but the rumour obstinately sticks and is still on Wikipedia. No, I do not own a château or a sprawling mansion, unlike other First Ladies before me, such as Carla Bruni-Sarzoky, Bernadette Chirac and Anne-Aymone Giscard d'Estaing. But our council house looked like a palace to me the first time I stepped over the threshold. I had just turned four, we were moving from a tower block full of council flats, and suddenly we were in a house with a garden. So even though we were four to a room, yes, it was a palace.

I really did have all the faults for the role: not married, not wealthy, working class and working … It really wasn't very First Lady-like of me at all. Critics will say what they will but I smashed my glass ceiling the day I set foot on the red carpet. I smashed through it so hard that thousands of shards of glass cut me deeply on the way.

I put my heart and soul into my new role from the very first day I arrived at the Élysée Palace. I immediately met with Carla Bruni-Sarkozy's former team and asked her team leader and each of her assistants what they had in mind going forward. Though my drama queen reputation had preceded me, they all decided to stay on board. All of them. I do not think they came to regret it, far from it. We lived through some intense moments together. With their precious help, I got stuck in straight away prepping the President's trip to the US. I was asked to choose a gift for Michelle Obama. I chose products that had been made in Corrèze, a handbag and beauty products – a nod to the Corrèze region – at a fraction of the usual cost of official gifts.

A few days after the election, I flew off to Washington alongside the President. When I climbed onto the private presidential plane I understood why the press had nicknamed it 'Air Sarkozy': inside the plane, there is a large room, a bathroom, an office for the President and a room for meetings and lunches. Eleven seats around

the table. Most of the time the seats are filled by ministers, the Chief of Staff and the Diplomatic Adviser – both
worthy men. Laurent Fabius aside, you hardly needed to
be an expert to see that the new Cabinet ministers did
not have what it took. What I heard was disheartening to
say the least. I observed them in silence, wondering how
any of them could have been appointed ministers. Their
appointment was all about balancing factions, gender,
regions and parties. Few of them were there because of
a particular aptitude for the role. That much was abun-
dantly obvious to the former political journalist I still was
deep down. The press was very critical of their amateurism and I might well have written the same thing had I
still been working for *Paris-Match*'s political pages. But
I kept my mouth shut.

In Washington, I had the strange feeling that I was
an actress in a film that I was also a spectator of. The
ambassador's wife took me under her wing and organised meetings with the US press. The media was curious
about me: I was 'the French woman who is still working'
and 'the unmarried First Lady'. Still, in their eyes I was
also a colleague and it went off smoothly.

I was not included in the Presidents' programme
because it was not a state visit: François Hollande was
in the US for a NATO council. I realised that I would
leave the US without getting a chance to meet Barack

Obama, a privilege that would have made me very proud. I was in the First Ladies' programme. I keenly appreciated how much of an honour it was to be welcomed by Michelle Obama at the White House. She waited for us in the hall and greeted each of us individually – there were eight First Ladies in total. She embraced us as if we were friends – US-style.

Michelle Obama is the person who most impressed me over the last couple of years.

Physically, to begin with. Even though I was wearing very high heels I only reached her shoulders. As for elegance and poise, I didn't even come close. She was tall, beautiful and much slimmer than in pictures. She stretched her long arms with a swan's grace.

She radiated charisma, she had a real aura about her.

Michelle Obama was the perfect hostess and showed us around the White House before lunch. I had to pinch myself to realise where I was. I kept reminding myself to enjoy every second of these unique moments that fate was bestowing upon me.

The US First Lady had done her research about each of us. She and I had a brief exchange about my work with the Danielle Mitterrand Foundation. In shaky English, I asked her about her programme to combat obesity. Meanwhile, she confessed that it had taken her a year to find her feet in this First Lady role that is not quite like any other. Everyone had already forgotten that when she first became First Lady, she made sensational statements about her husband's dirty socks, something which did not go down well with Americans – who took a while to adjust to the first black couple in the White House.

Ever mindful of etiquette, Michelle Obama granted the same discussion time to each First Lady. Conversation was fairly mundane. I observed her and wondered about her – a woman who from the outside was so perfect and impenetrable. Was she enjoying this encounter or was she merely playing a role that had already been written, in which going off-script was simply not an option? I thought of how she had given up a high-flying career as a lawyer to serve her husband's career. She could have earned millions of dollars and worked on high-profile cases. But there she was, waxing lyrical about her kitchen garden, which she would show us around later. The vegetables on our plates came from her garden, the cooks had done wonders with them but the portions were so small that I was still a little hungry after lunch. I had a hunger for a lot of things, in fact. How I would have loved to have a proper conversation with her! I would have given a lot to find out who was under that perfect mask of hers, to find out what she really thought of being First Lady – a role that has far more rules and constraints in the US than in France, but which is also a position with real status.

The next morning I found out on the internet that I was now being nicknamed the 'First Girlfriend'. After a US broadsheet had used the expression, the French press had taken it on and was having a field day with it. It made me uncomfortable, I felt like I had outgrown being a 'girlfriend', especially after seven years of living with François, but such is the media game.

Mid-morning, I joined Michelle Obama in Chicago. She took us to the suburb she had grown up in. She wanted to show us an organisation that took care of under-privileged children and gave them access to all sorts of activities their parents would never be able to afford for them.

After the visit, Michelle Obama gave a speech to the other First Ladies and an audience of young people. It showed true political commitment and she bowled me over: 'You might not all become Presidents, but you can become doctors, lawyers … Barack and I became what we are by working hard. Give yourselves the means to become what you want to become!' Michelle Obama was inspiring. In later official trips, when I visited orphanages in South Africa or in India's poorest quarters I repeated her words, trying to recapture the strength she instilled in them. The idea that you should not give up simply because you were not born in the right place was a message that really struck a chord with me. Luck is something you deserve. And once you've earned it, you should share it.

In the evening, we had dinner with a dozen women, including two of Michelle Obama's best friends, in a Chicago museum. The setting was magical. Michelle Obama had pulled out all the stops.

François had flown off to Camp David early the previous evening – the First Ladies were not joining their spouses on that leg of the trip. After dinner, I was left to my own devices – in our hotel suite guarded by an impressive number of US security officers.

Back in Washington, a French journalist living in the US whom I had known for years invited me to dinner. She said she wanted to write a book about First Ladies. I made it clear that I was agreeing to dinner only, not to her book. We talked about our lives, I told her about my children and shared a few of my worries and concerns. At the end of the dinner, she confessed that she was working on a book about me… I was alarmed: 'We had an agreement: this dinner was off the record, right?' She promised me it was. Besides, she had not taken any notes or recorded our conversation. I wasn't worried.

Two months later I found out she had betrayed me. Not only had she used the information I had shared with her in complete confidence, but she had also distorted it entirely. I took her to court over her book, *La Frondeuse*.[20] At the

---

20  *The Troublemaker.*

hearing, the author implied that I had shared intimate details of previous romantic involvements. A barefaced lie.

That series of books about me revealing my alleged neurotic personality, by journalists I had not even met for the most part, was one of the worst ordeals I have ever had to go through. In the first few months of the presidential mandate they were a dime a dozen. The first one to come out was penned by a former deputy director at *Le Monde* and set the 'standard' for the rest. The title of the book alone, *La favorite*,[21] was insulting. He had never met me. I did not even know his name. He made liberal use of 'poetic' licence, fabricated, attacked and misrepresented me. A despicable exercise in 'style'. It is very strange to experience the reinvention and fictionalisation of your life. I stood by, powerless, as a character was born who had my name, my face, my life, but who was not me – it was all make-believe.

I was alone. An aloneness that looked a lot like loneliness. Not a single woman spoke out in my defence – and feminists were noticeable in their absence. François' response was pure indifference, as if the problem did not concern him. I was being saddled with a vile nickname and it did not bother him in the slightest.

Meanwhile, a colleague at *Paris-Match* came up with

---

21  *The King's Mistress.*

another bon mot and made sure it circulated widely – I had become François Hollande's 'Rottweiler', his watchdog. The catchphrase became the latest fad. Malicious gossip is a deplorable disease, though between friends it is often benign. But the consequences are tenfold when – as is possible nowadays – you can play that cruel little game with the entire world on social networks. The 'network society' breeds what US researchers call 'cyberbullying' and a 'culture of humiliation'.

My skin was not thick enough back then to reject the venom – that came later. The onslaught was harsh and I felt besmirched. It was my Achilles' heel. I tried to hide from my children just how much I was affected – not far from drowning – by all those books and all that sarcasm, because they too took it badly.

Having learned from a young age to fight back against adversity distorted my vision of the world. By dint of seeing enemies everywhere, I ended up making a lot of them.

It didn't matter that I knew I was not the only person whose reputation had been smeared. I remember Carla Bruni-Sarkozy's tears at the handover of power. At one point or another the foreign First Ladies had all had to put up with ill treatment at the hands of the press. There were recurrent rebukes regardless of the country and personality of the First Lady in question. The spouses of heads of state are almost always suspected of meddling in their husbands' affairs, to have ambition for two and to unduly spend public money. Their reputation is tarnished by rumour.

One of the First Ladies confessed that it pained her to hear people say she had 'got her claws into a President' because she was twenty years younger than her husband… At least no one could accuse me of being attracted to power! My partner wasn't even President of the General Council when I met him.

One evening, the wife of the Japanese Prime Minister Abe had me in stitches with the story of how she was lambasted for supporting one of her friends in the Senate elections. Hearing about her misfortunes consoled me somewhat about my regrettable tweet. She told me with great humour how every time she expressed her views publicly, the media unleashed its venom. In fairness, she didn't think twice about saying she was opposed to nuclear power, when her husband's decisions were leading the country in the opposite direction…

I developed a friendship with the wife of former Malian President Traoré. Though I no longer have an official role, Mintou Traoré continues to regularly check in on me. She was the one who welcomed me to Mali on my first solo trip in May 2013. At the same time, the Malian President was in France with François. There was something symbolic about that: men go out onto the military field, while we women are in the humanitarian field. We flew to Gao in a military Transall plane with the members of Operation Serval. It was not a world I was familiar with and I was struck for the first time by the true nobility of the members of the military. I was moved to see them on the field, at the service of a population traumatised by jihadist acts of violence.

We visited a school that had nothing: no tables or chairs, no books, no pencils. We brought textbooks. We also visited young mothers who had just given birth in the resourceless local hospital. One of them was resting after delivering twins, a girl and a boy. They had only been born two hours previously and did not yet have names. Mintou placed them in my arms and with an air of authority she declared: 'He's François and she's Valérie!' This got a laugh out of everyone. It is one of my favourite pictures of that trip. My shiny eyes hint at the tears of emotion I am holding back.

If those two are really called François and Valérie, I only wish that a happier fate is in store for them than ours…

Everywhere I went, I had to say a few words, sometimes even make a short speech. It wasn't something I knew how to do so I improvised. At my own modest level, I began to understand the pleasure that François felt in experiencing such moments.

After the visit, we had lunch with the soldiers and their commander under a tent at the military camp, in heat of at least 45 degrees Celsius. A storm was brewing, torrential rain started pouring down. Everyone was running around frantically, as it was the first rain of the season. The journalists were amused. They said I had acquired François' power: to make it rain wherever he went – as it had on his inauguration day! The elements really were against us, the wind rose and truly showed us what it could do – we had to move our departure forward.

I visited the hospital and orphanage in Bamako. What I saw there will haunt me forever: dozens of infants suffering from respiratory distress or extremely premature newborns. Their chances of survival were in jeopardy.

Once we had returned to France, a medical mission was sent out to try to understand why there were so many infants with serious medical conditions in that hospital.

Another sad sight that will stay with me is the terrible conditions disabled children were faced with at the crèche: they were all sat in a row on the floor of a squalid corridor, irrespective of their various disabilities.

My goal during my trip to Mali had been to ask the government to reconsider the cancellation of adoption agreements, a change of policy affecting seventy French families. There was a new law in Mali banning adoption by foreigners, and because it was retroactive, families who had celebrated the good news of a child on the way had seen their hopes cruelly crushed. Before leaving France, I had talked several times to a French organisation[22] working to break the adoption deadlock in Mali. I had seen the distress of the French families involved and had promised to help them – with the President's green light. Unfortunately, once I got to Mali, it became clear that we would have to wait until after the Malian elections.

With the help of the wife of the new President, I went back on the offensive. Things are now moving forward – slowly but surely. The families still give me news of what is going on. I have not given up hope.

At a press conference just before we left Mali, a journalist asked Mrs Traoré to comment on France's commitment to Mali. 'When a man goes to bed,' she replied, 'he has not yet made a decision. He reaches it with the woman who sleeps next to him. And the woman he sleeps with is Valérie.' In the highly charged atmosphere of the press conference, her explosive answer made us all laugh and dispelled some of the tension.

Mali is a land bursting with emotion. I understood the emotion François had felt when he went there in his role as the army's Commander in Chief after the French military operation. But not when he publicly claimed it was 'the happiest day in [his] political career'. I wasted no time messaging him to say he should feel ashamed

---

22  *Collectif adoption Mali.*

of himself: 'If the happiest day in your political career is not the day that the people of France made you President, then they were wrong to do so.' I admit I didn't humour him that day. But was there still anyone who really dared to confront him – among his pack of courtesans, of 'complimenters'? Regrettably, there was not.

François had become unable to handle criticism. It was easier to keep your mouth shut than to be faced with a barrage of abuse.

*Late spring 2014...*

Summer of 2014 is drawing closer and rumours are circulating that Hollande and Gayet will soon make their relationship official. They are allegedly still seeing each other. François makes the first move – by text message – assuring me for the umpteenth time that the rumour is just that, a rumour, he swears that the affair is over, that it is me he wants back and the girl means nothing to him.

I have heard it all before – unfaithful men have been singing that tune since time immemorial.

Every single day, François asks to see me. The pressure never lets up. I have stopped answering. Because I do not know where the boundary lies between his truths and untruths, I cannot rebuild the small nugget of trust without which, as I discovered, all human relationships hit a wall.

For the third time, François promises he will publicly deny that he is involved with the actress. For the third time, he fails to do so. Is it because he is afraid he will end up alone that he has a finger in every pie? Is he keeping communication channels open with me because my freedom scares him?

He did eventually get around to refuting the wedding rumour, on 12 August, his sixtieth birthday – which he asked me to spend with him, adding: 'You are the one who should say "I do" to me.'

I HAVE TO turn over to a new chapter. A beautiful quote by Tahar Ben Jelloun, 'The silence of your loved one is a quiet crime', keeps me going. I know it by heart and I repeat it to myself every day.

I cannot say which of the two of us is suffering more. He tries to find out how I am, through friends or through my youngest son, whom he still sees. He wants to know what I am up to, who I see, what I think. He asks everyone why I do not want to see him any more. When we had dinner together for the first time after the separation statement was issued, he said: 'I won't mention your book, because I don't want you to think that I am coming back to you because of that.'

I do not want to hear about his life, I do not want to know what is going on at the Élysée. My TV is always off and I do not read the papers. Every news stand I walk past is like a radioactive site to me – it is full of noxious poison.

The world I lock myself in gets smaller and smaller, it is a fragile little bubble. I try to fight back – but I have lost the frantic, desperate energy of the first few weeks. Apparently it is known as the after-effect. As if the first effect did not hurt enough. Throw more my way. One cheek. And then the other. Two slaps in the face. Just to even things out. I barely had time to get back on my feet before I took another blow.

François hurt me deeply. I admit I do sometimes miss him, I miss the past, I miss our love, our carefree passion, the hours when everything seemed easy, when the colours were more vivid and the air was easier to breathe. But the past never comes back. Or when it does, it comes back in painful bursts that overwhelm me and threaten to crush me: the past is tenacious and it refuses to die – especially the pre-Élysée past when François was a different man. Or rather when he was himself.

His messages talk of love. He writes that I am his whole

life, that he is nothing without me. Are his messages heartfelt? Does he even believe what he himself writes? Or am I the latest tantrum of a man who cannot bear to lose? He writes that he will win me back, as if I was an election. I know him well now: perhaps he believes that if he manages to win me back, to repeat an impossible feat, he may also manage to win back the heart of the French people – even though he is the most unpopular President of France's Fifth Republic.

All my trust in him has died. For the French people, of course, it is a whole other matter. I can only bear witness to the fact that power changes people. I cannot recognise the François I loved with wild abandon in the man who treated me with such contempt and now reserves that contempt for his collaborators. Day after day, under the weight of his responsibilities, I saw him lose his humanity, drunk on power, incapable of empathy.

It struck me at dinner with his inner circle from the Voltaire year of the École Nationale d'administration: they had been waiting for power for thirty years. They finally had it, and they felt like demigods, full of arrogance.

I also remember a comment he made during a walk which really shocked me. We were talking about his Foreign Affairs Minister, Laurent Fabius. A man who, in 1987, had become France's youngest ever Prime Minister, at thirty-seven.

'It's awful for him, he's wasted his life,' François said.

'What makes you say that?' I asked.

'He never became President.'

'But that doesn't mean he wasted his life,' I protested. 'He seems happy in what he does, and with his partner … What about you, are you happy?'

'No.'

My days go by slowly, the President's text messages mark time.

One.

Three.

Five.

I can't help but read them. I end up caving in and I answer his last message. He responds immediately. The whole song and dance all over again, on an endless loop. We are going nowhere with these messages and the whole thing exhausts me. His words have no more value for me. I put an end to it. Until next time. I want to get some distance from François, whom I do not understand any more, and from the Élysée – I never even drive past it these days, I would sooner make a detour.

I am prepared to go just about anywhere to escape from this knot of sadness. Which is part of the reason why I immediately agree when *Paris-Match* asks me to do an assignment in Nigeria to try to trace the school-girls kidnapped by Boko Haram. As it is, every day I try to rally public opinion for their cause – with my own means, mostly via my Twitter account or through media coverage. When my newspaper suggests the reportage, I reply that I am prepared to leave that very second, if necessary – quite literally. But Nigeria blocks the project by denying us visas.

In fact, I have only just returned from a trip to the Democratic Republic of the Congo with Dr Mukwege to provide support to street kids and women who have been victims of rape. The thought of going away again fills me with newfound energy.

As was the case on my trip to Haiti with *Secours populaire*, meeting the most destitute reminds me of what really matters.

Humanitarian work is sometimes criticised for the media coverage it comes hand in hand with. Who is right and who is wrong? A few years ago, reporting for *Paris-Match*, I visited a refugee camp in Ethiopia along with opera singer Barbara Hendricks. For several years, this charismatic and talented woman put her fame at the service of humanitarian causes. Barbara Hendricks was born in a segregated America and it had left a permanent mark on her – as if she had been branded. She turned that humiliation into strength. She moved mountains with the sheer power of her beliefs. She cannot bear the idea that a child can be born without a fair chance. We both share that hatred of injustice and my experience as a First Lady only confirmed to me that these trips are useful. They help focus energy and give local teams much-needed and much-deserved visibility.

With that in mind, I have a meeting with the heads of Action Contre la Faim. We discuss the possibility of a visit to a country ravaged by war before the end of the year.

Dangerous areas do not scare me. I did not bat an eyelid at the thought of travelling to Nigeria.

Perhaps it is fair to say that I am a bit reckless. My life has lost its meaning. Without my children, I do not know what I would have become. I need to find my way again, and to do so I am more than willing to take a few risks.

During the meeting, we discuss my trip to India back in January, only one day after the separation statement François Hollande dictated to the AFP. One of the representatives from Action Contre la Faim was on that trip with me. She praises me warmly for my courage: 'You resisted media pressure and were very giving. I have not seen many people like you in the field.'

I went on that trip to India with my friend Charlotte Valandrey, an actress who is HIV positive and has had a heart transplant. The word 'survival' has real meaning to her – something she has talked about in several moving books. She was there to tell me how to recover and regain control over myself. Her words soothed me.

In January, I had been thrown to sharks in international waters, as if I was completely worthless. Refusing to cancel my trip to India was a way of showing the small circle of people celebrating my eviction from the Élysée that I still had dignity. That I did not deserve François Hollande's scorn. I also wanted to show François that I would cope without him.

It was not just my friend Charlotte: many more shared their strength with me. The joy of the children of the Bombay slums was communicative. A fortnight ago, a magazine ran a picture of that trip. I am sat cross-legged on the floor with a little girl on my lap. My hand rests on her little leg and her hand rests on mine. In that moment, Paris truly was million miles away. I was happy to be there.

I also remember a trip to South Africa when I was First Lady and how the orphanage children made me dance with them. I was more than willing. When it comes to dancing to frenzied beats, I have never needed to be asked twice!

The same thing happened in Burundi, where I had been invited to attend a conference by Mary Robinson. In the end, the musicians encouraged me to dance along to the sound of their drums.

Generally speaking, during official trips, I was always happy to get a chance to escape from the 'Madame programme'. When a visit to a museum or sightseeing was suggested, I declined. I wanted to get off the beaten track.

What I most remember of my trip to Burundi, and of an earlier trip I went on alone as First Lady, in July 2013, is the face of a little boy called Olivier. I met him when I was visiting a centre for young boys living on the street. The centre kept them for six months and helped them reintegrate in society. During my visit, the boys and I sat in a circle. Only three of them spoke, Olivier was one of them. Some of those boys had something very special, you could tell straight away, and again Olivier was one of them.

'I don't want to go and live on the street again,' he said, 'I want to study, I want to become a doctor. What will happen to me if I go back on the street?'

After the visit, I asked the wife of the ambassador for a favour. I asked her to keep an eye on how Olivier was doing – just until I could find a solution for him. Two days after I got back to Paris, a childless couple, both of them doctors, agreed to finance his education and board with a family in Burundi. That way, Olivier would not be uprooted and could fulfil his dream. Over the last two years, Olivier has made amazing progress in school. The couple sponsoring him speaks to him every week on Skype. If all goes well – fingers crossed – in eight years he will come to France to study medicine.

Too many children do not have the same luck. In only twenty months at the Élysée, I saw countless children's centres and hospitals filled with sick patients. It is enough to make you feel completely powerless. The efforts you are making feel like a drop in the ocean. Until you remember that the ocean is just that: accumulated drops. Little by little, drop by drop, we can do more. A single drop of water makes a difference – and it is missed if it is not there.

There is Olivier, but there is also Solenne, whom I met through ELA,[23] an organisation sponsored by Zinedine Zidane. The head of ELA was the first person to ask for my help, right after the 'La Rochelle tweet' – at a time when I felt like I had caught cholera and was so contagious no one wanted to get anywhere near me. He explained that leukodystrophies were a group of rare genetic disorders, which cause a terrible and irreversible degeneration of the nervous system.

I agreed to do a spelling test in a school, to help raise awareness of the disease and encourage donations. In Year 10 of a school in the thirteenth arrondissement in Paris, I read out the dictation in front of a swarm of photographers and cameras. Solenne was there in her wheelchair, along with her parents. She was a pretty little blonde girl

---

23 European Leukodystrophies Association.

with a sense of humour. The students in the first row were crying. I held my own tears back because, after meeting many parents of disabled children, I knew that what they wanted was support, not compassion.

Solenne later wrote to me to say that moment had changed her life. The few lines of the dictation took her two hours to write because her motor skills were so limited but, for the first time in her life, she was the centre of attention. I kept her letter like a treasure, and wrote back to her. I invited Solenne to the children's Christmas at the Élysée that year, even though invitations were meant to be only for children under twelve. I wanted that Christmas to be special for both Solenne and the young orphaned girls. I wanted to find an imaginative and personal present, rather than a formal present, to mark the occasion. As I knew that Solenne cared about her appearance, I asked the President's Chief of Staff permission to buy six bags by designer Vanessa Bruno – a brand teenagers in posh Parisian neighbourhoods go crazy for.

'That's expensive, why don't you get copies instead?' she replied. Proof that attending the École nationale d'administration doesn't necessarily make up for lack of common sense.

'I can't do that,' I said. 'We are at the Élysée Palace, we can't buy counterfeit products and give them out as gifts!'

She may have had a point about the price, but the

Élysée's attempts to be 'normal' and reduce spending can sometimes lead to strange decisions being made. For instance, on the grounds that it was free, a show featuring Asterix and Obelix came to the Élysée. The producer had one condition: that the red carpet be rolled out for the actors – in full Asterix and Obelix guise – and that the President welcome them in person, on the front steps of the Élysée, as if they were heads of state... I stopped François just in time, fearing that he would be the object of ridicule. Then again, it would hardly have been more of an embarrassment than images of a President hiding under a full-face helmet.

In any event, we found a free solution for the girls: they got their authentic Vanessa Bruno bags, generously donated by the creator herself when she found out who the presents were for.

With her mother's help, I was also able to surprise Solenne by picking her up after school to take her for tea at the Élysée Palace. My security guards happily agreed to carry Solenne up the stairs.

Solenne and I have kept in touch over the last two years. I saw her ten days ago, she was ecstatic about getting her handi-dog after a two-year wait. She went to Alençon with her father to tame her new friend, who would be helping her in her everyday life. A €15,000 friend, because it is very expensive to train handi-dogs and then teach the two new companions to interact with one another. All this is made possible thanks to donations, which are infinitely precious.

Over the months, I realised that I had a role to play as a First Lady, appealing to people's generosity to help fund the organisation. The disability requires sophisticated equipment which is not fully reimbursed by French social security.

I am reminded of young Théo in his motorised wheelchair. Théo had both arms and both legs amputated when he was six following a very rare form of meningitis. His idol, Philippe Croizon, also had a motorised wheelchair – as he had also lost his limbs, as the result of electrocution. I see Philippe Croizon on television and hear him speak on the radio. He is a hero to me and impresses me with his strength: he swam across the Channel and is now planning to swim four straights separating the five continents. When Nicolas Sarkozy was President, he awarded him the Légion d'honneur. Philippe's fame is what helps him find the sponsors who allow him to live out his dream.

I pestered François to see Philippe but he would not. In the end, I invited Philippe to come and see me at the Élysée, and made sure François would drop in at the end of the meeting. Philippe, his partner, his agent, and I had been talking for an hour when François joined us. He was affable and cheerful, as he knows how to be.

Over dinner that evening, I asked François what he had thought of Croizon.

'I don't like disabled people who trade on their disability.'

I was gobsmacked. What had happened to the man I had known who could be so sensitive, who knew how to find soothing and tender words? How could he have become so harsh, insensitive and cutting – a cynic who aims where it hurts? He knew about my father's ordeal and Philippe Croizon's suffering was far worse. I reminded François that disability benefits were only €790 a month. When I was growing up, it was even less, and there were eight of us to feed on those benefits – until my mother found a job as a cashier. François did not answer. He had already moved on to another dossier in his head.

I stayed in touch with Philippe Croizon, someone who, unlike François, knows how to communicate his strength to others. Philippe continues to check in on me, he worries about me. We went to Vichy together to support Théo in his swimming training. Théo wants to become a champion, like his idol Philippe: his dream is to take part in the Paralympics. To have met this twelve-year-old boy is to know what it is to be exceptional – his determination is beyond belief. He has now been a runner-up in three junior competitions in France.

I can certainly say that I experienced some precious

moments and that I met some truly extraordinary people when I was First Lady at the Élysée. But not one of those experiences or people were in politics.

When I was dismissed, I publicly thanked the Élysée staff. The cooks, the florists, the doctors, the maîtres d', and so many more... All of them helped me through many a difficult moment. I want to make special mention of one of the maîtres d', who always knew how to brighten up my day. Not to mention my former team: all five of them showed me affection and I really did develop a strong bond with them.

This summer Fort de Brégançon will be open to the public. It is the summer residence of the President of France, but the current President will not spend his holiday there after our separation. It is all over the media and the press has decided to retrace the history of presidential holidays. Out comes – again – the fabricated story about some pillows I allegedly ordered two years ago, when we arrived at the Élysée!

That summer, François sent me on a recce with a former photographer hired by the Élysée. The idea was for me to describe the place to him and discover whether there was a solution to the paparazzi problem. I spent half a day visiting the port. Save setting up two large partitions on the beach, I requested no changes. But only a few days later I found out, thanks to a rumour doing the rounds on the internet and in the press, that I had supposedly ordered luxury cushions and outdoor furniture, racking up a bill of tens of thousands of euros!

Our first holidays started with that public scandal. What an irresistible fantasy: a parvenue who thinks she is the next Marie Antoinette and spends public money on tantrums was too good to be *un*true. I asked the Élysée repeatedly to issue a statement denying this tall story – it may have been against me but it impacted the President too. Nothing was done.

François was reluctant to upset the press, even when it transformed hearsay into so-called information. To him, the news is a river that carries everything with it, fact and fiction, and there is no use in swimming against the current. He preferred to find out which way the wind was blowing and play with it.

Meanwhile, the message from the Élysée was not to take the whole thing too seriously. Two years later, I had proof that the poison was still seeping out since the press reported that the Élysée had erased the traces of my tantrum after my departure. Obviously there had to be an explanation to the fact that any visitors to the fort would not find anything – neither overpriced cushions, nor garden furniture carved out of precious wood!

Our summer holidays back in August 2012 did get off to a bad start. I had to put up with the masquerade of our departure by train. The holidays of 'President Normal' were dramatically staged by the Élysée's PR service, in front of dozens of cameras and photographers assembled on the platform at the Gare de Lyon station, in front of our train. The whole thing was ridiculous in my opinion; I hated putting on the whole show. It shows in the pictures: I look like I got out of bed on the wrong side, I am frowning and my features are frozen.

We did not crave the same things: François wanted a walkabout or two, he had been missing them since his election, while I was expecting a little bit of privacy after a two-year political campaign. If you stay within Fort de Brégançon you can hide away, and the garden and the view are magnificent. Suddenly, everything seemed to calm down and it was such a pleasure. Though the rooms were dark, he and I spent lovely moments together inside the fort. I had brought a couple of dozen books among the new titles that were coming out in September, to prepare my book column. Every day, François received phone calls from heads of state and the Fort's aide-de-camp brought him new dossiers. He worked for hours while I read. We were glad to spend time together when we had finished our work.

Unfortunately, we could not set foot outside without being chased by a pack of journalists. I asked them repeatedly to leave us alone. But François would tell them not to mind me: 'Go ahead.'

He was still glowing from the halo of the campaign, when his every move – a rushed factory visit, a muddy farmyard, a supermarket aisle – was followed by a horde of photographers and journalists with their cameras, feverishly collecting precious snippets uttered by the candidate. But now that he had become President his image was that of a man who spent his time on the beach, walking around in a polo shirt, followed by a sullen woman. No matter that the truth was quite the opposite: he didn't stop working and we also managed to finally regain some moments of calm and intimacy. The illusions that images can create...

We left the fort from the back, by boat, and managed to steal a few moments and escape the paparazzi, to cycle around Porquerolles and walk around the magical islands of Port-Cros. All the French Presidents before François Hollande were entitled to their rest. The French will remember images of a tanned Pompidou lounging on a deck chair with his wife, of François Mitterrand in a light suit and straw boater at his property in Latche.

A single picture of François at his desk in the famous office of the General de Gaulle would have been enough to clamp the gossips' mouths shut. In fact, at the end of his stay François wanted to organise a meeting to discuss the budget with Jean-Marc Ayrault and both the Minister of the Economy and the Budget Minister. But the Prime Minister was reluctant to leave his holiday home in

Brittany and François did not insist… The meeting would no doubt have helped lift the press sulk and might have mitigated the negative opinion the public had at the start of his presidency. Then again, politics would be so simple if it was only about images.

By September 2012 François had already started his freefall in the polls – it was a slap in the face. He saw a causal effect between that and his holiday and decided to go from one extreme to the other: no more holidays or even weekends. For years he had been on a media drip and was easily swayed by everything the media commented on – written or spoken.

It was in the press that I learned the following year that we would not go back to Brégançon and that he had complained of having spent nightmarish holidays there. Once again, it was in the press that I heard we would only be spending a few days in La Lanterne over the summer of 2013 by way of a holiday.

Last year, I decided to take my children on holiday for a week in Greece, in a hotel I booked through a discount holiday website. I was probably the first First Lady to have purchased a low-cost holiday when all the leaders in the world were offering to loan splendid properties to the French President.

It was only once I had left the Élysée and no longer had to answer to anyone that I finally felt free to do as I pleased with that austerity rule. I said yes to a break in the sun with my friends Valérie and Saïda. We went to a beautiful hotel for eight days, off-season. I needed to get away from Paris, I needed to feel protected. I needed to be 'elsewhere'. I want to thank them: they did me a world of good at that moment. I know what I owe them and a few others I will not name in this book because they are better off remaining anonymous. I know the strength of friendship between women and it saved me.

The misunderstandings between us started to build up after we got back from Brégançon. In autumn 2012, I started to wonder why the man I loved so passionately was gradually distancing himself from me. I opened up about it to a friend, whose answer, if rather blunt, contained an element of truth: 'It seems to me that his love is linked to his popularity ratings.'

The primaries, followed by the presidential campaign, were the peak of his life. I remember that a few days before the second round it was as if François was levitating, carried by the crowd, inhabited by collective energy. Once he was elected his popularity ratings became of utmost concern to him. It brings him back to that kick he got – like getting a hard-drug hit – from meeting the cheering crowds who were carried by everything he embodied.

With each new poll I saw him diminish. And without fail, immediately afterwards his attitude towards me would harden a little more each time. He needed someone to blame his fall in popularity on. He could not be responsible, so I had to be, and others.

Officially he pretended he wasn't affected but that was very obviously untrue. I became his lightning rod – for absolutely everything that happened to him. Unemployment soared and I bore the consequences. For every false note from a ministry, every factory closure, I knew I was in for trouble: he was increasingly distant and cutting. With everyone. Everything was wrong. Down to the menus – which he chose himself – and the bread that was never fresh enough. Everything was my fault.

For months, his popularity dropped inexorably in opinion polls. The first months of his five-year term were a succession of air-pockets. He had always praised my political flair. So, every evening when I saw him, I tried to explain what I felt was wrong in terms of PR and policies. But he did not want to hear about the mistakes. He shut down and got angry. The plunge was fast and no doubt harsh. The amateurism image did a lot of damage, not to mention the various 'bum notes'. In his eyes the Prime Minister, Jean-Marc Ayrault, whom he himself had chosen, was starting to have all the flaws in the world. Minus that of disloyalty. Was there still someone who found favour with him? All I heard was criticism of this or that person.

Early on, when François started mentioning Manuel Valls, his Minister of the Interior, as a replacement for Jean-Marc Ayrault, I was quick to warn him: 'You know that if you pick Valls, you are giving him the car and the key,' I said. 'And he's going to clear off with the lot. If you are in a weak position in 2017, he is going to call for primaries so that he can stand.'

'If I am in a weak position I won't run.'

'Yes, you will, you'll get back on your feet and you are a brilliant campaigner.' I still believed in him.

Some evenings, I made good resolutions. I promised myself I would not talk to him about the problems of that day. I tried to find positive subjects, and when I failed I kept my mouth shut or spoke of things concerning everyday life. I was wasting my time: he took over the conversation and attacked some of his advisers or his ministers. He was losing his clear-sightedness and cool – which had always been his strength until then. He could not see what was happening. I made a mistake at that moment: I failed to see that he needed something else. That his distress called for reassurance and sweetness. Seeking refuge in the arms of an actress who thought he was 'magical' and gazed at him like a young girl in love was no doubt more pleasurable for him – and it certainly was the easy way.

Going from the fairy tale that was the electoral campaign

to the barrenness of power was a real shock. One Saturday evening at La Lanterne, a few weeks after the election, we were watching images of Johnny Hallyday's concert at the Stade de France. He was mesmerised; it was as though he had been hypnotised. I could read his mind easily: 'You miss it, don't you?' He smiled: yes, he did. He and I knew what it was all about. I had covered so many electoral campaigns and accompanied him to countless meetings: the walka-bouts, the warmth of the crowds cheering, of the murmurs of assent and the laughter, his voice cajoling and winning the crowd over, the studied body language of candidates… I was one of the rare journalists – and at times I really was the only one – who had covered his first steps in politics. I could never get enough of his speeches. When our close relationship turned into love he would send me hidden messages in those speeches that only I could pick up on.

Within the Élysée, François did not distinguish between those who were by his side for his sake and to serve the state and those who had only joined him to serve their own career and use his influence to their advantage. I was especially wary of Aquilino Morelle. The President's spe-cial adviser was certainly that … special. We simply did not get on. He was still the campaign director of a rival candidate during the primaries, when he came to sell him-self to François at rue Cauchy… I have always abhorred duplicitous behaviour.

When François was appointed, Morelle became the man who wrote his speeches, or rather the draft versions of his speeches. François tore into him repeatedly in front of me when he came to our home during the campaign. Morelle felt humiliated and took his resentment out on me.

Once he had made it to the Élysée, Morelle took over the best office, the most beautiful car, and strutted up and down like a peacock. I heard several accounts of his methods and his behaviour, often against me. I spoke to François about it but he brushed my concerns about the things I had heard: 'Do you have any proof?'

'No, just first-hand accounts.'

That did not satisfy him.

Aquilino Morelle could not have been happier about my departure in January 2014. In fact, he helped pen the eighteen-word dismissal statement – cold contempt is very much his style. In May 2014, it was my turn to be thrilled at his forced resignation. All by himself, he tripped up on the laces of his custom-made shoes. No one would be shining his shoes any more. No more boot-licking for him. His vanity was his downfall.

I had already left the Élysée Palace when the Morelle scandal came to light – the adviser had been using public funds to bring a shoeshiner to the Élysée and to order custom-made shoes. Still, in spite of our separation I warned François of the consequences of the scandal. He failed to see just how serious it was. 'You can keep blinding yourself about Morelle, as you did for your Budget Minister, whose hidden accounts abroad were eventually brought to the public's attention … Either way, I can assure you that the consequences will be the same.' He replied that those were only anecdotes. 'If you think having a shoeshiner come to the Élysée is an anecdote,' I said, 'you really have changed. No point me even mentioning the lab money.'

I was probably not the only one to warn François because the message eventually sank in and Aquilino Morelle left the Élysée that very day.

As for the business of the Budget Minister in charge of combating tax fraud having hidden accounts abroad, the President did not see it coming. And yet it is one of the rare subjects which I took a firm stance on with François, repeatedly – as soon as the very first articles came out about it. My attempts to be heard were fruitless, he simply was not having any of it – always asking me the same question: 'Do you have proof?'

No, obviously I did not have any proof. But I had eyes and a good memory. The first red flag had come a few years earlier. At the time, I was presenting a political show on television and I witnessed with utter incredulity how docile he was in a debate with Marine Le Pen, the leader of the far-right party. My team and I were shocked: the Socialist MP was behaving with her as a teenager would with a Hollywood star – with complete deference.

Something was not right. When the press revealed that his bank account in Switzerland had been opened by a family friend, a far-right lawyer who was close to Marine Le Pen, the pieces of the jigsaw puzzle started to slot together.

I read the articles, listened to his defence: there was something dissonant. In December, during a Sunday lunch at the Valls', conversation moved to the Budget Minister and his Swiss bank account.

'It's awful for him,' said Manuel Valls, 'he can't sleep anymore.'

Without missing a beat, I replied: 'If he is not sleeping, he probably has a guilty conscience.'

'That's got nothing to do with it, his dignity is being attacked.'

Manuel Valls could have chosen another word than dignity. At the time, the debate on same-sex marriage was fuelling the 'fascist-sphere'. On the internet, the far right was fuming over the issue and I was name-called and insulted day in and day out – which made me somewhat less empathetic than the other guests to the Budget Minister's struggles with dignity. 'What about me? What are people doing if not attacking my dignity when they call me the First Whore of France?'

As one man, François, and his Minister of the Interior cried out: 'That's completely different!'

Completely different, indeed: he was a politician, draped in his honour, and I was a woman without a real role, a voodoo doll to be insulted freely and dragged in the mud. I did not bother arguing. I was convinced that the Budget Minister's head would get the chop. 'I am sure he is lying,' I insisted.

We all stuck to our guns. The two men were protecting the Budget Minister because he was one of them, a politician and a friend. At the end of the conversation, Manuel Valls said about him: 'You hold on, you hold on, until the moment when you just have to let go.'

TWO WEEKS LATER, when we were relaxing at home at rue Cauchy, the Budget Minister asked to see François urgently. He arrived within the hour; I was the one who opened the door to him. I offered him a tea with honey and lemon, which he accepted. I poured it and retired to our room to give them some privacy. I came out to say goodbye to him before he left. As soon as I had closed the door behind him, I grilled François: 'What did he want?'

'Nothing in particular,' he said.

'That can't be, he wouldn't come and take up the President's time on a Sunday just to have tea.'

'He is expecting more news to emerge.'

I did not get any more information out of him. Meanwhile, that moment was François' window of opportunity to seal his fate and forestall upcoming revelations. Two and a half months later, on 19 March 2013, when the Paris public prosecutor announced the launch of proceedings against the Budget Minister for 'laundering the proceeds of tax fraud', the minister resigned. It came as a brutal shock to François. Did he really remain incredulous until the very end? Why did he not take drastic action as soon as the minister came to our home that Sunday? François dislikes police cases, dossiers and rumours. Perhaps he did not want to believe it. When I saw François, he served up his customary sentence: 'You were right, but how did you know he was lying?'

I could not understand how he could be so blind or naive. And yet I was fooled by François' lies, as he looked me in the eye. We all see what we want to see.

The case was a devastating one. François clammed up. No one could get him out of that catatonic state. His closest advisers came to me for help. They were at a loss as to how to help him bounce back from the whole affair. One of his collaborators confessed that he had had it with the way the President handled things – he described it as 'working in Bcc'. François was the same with me, increasingly retreating into silence and opacity. I felt like furniture. If that. His popularity ratings took another plunge. He considered a major Cabinet reshuffle, including the departure of his Prime Minister Jean-Marc Ayrault. He reshuffled the entire Cabinet before changing his mind again. He does not know what a final decision is.

It took us a while to emerge from that dark time, The Élysée had become hell. In the first weeks following the election, I had wanted to take part in all the events. It is a journalist's dream: to walk through the looking-glass. I got over the excitement of it and hardly ever attended honours ceremonies after that. Instead, I made time for what matters to me: humanitarian work, children and social work. The advisers' games, the power plays, the bad-mouthing … I now knew how it worked. I had seen enough. Besides, François was not keen for me to interfere in that game, or for me to accompany him on public outings.

In fairness, at times he had a revival of tenderness towards me, because he thought I was beautiful on that particular day or that particular hour. During those moments he looked at me with shiny eyes again, took my hand furtively, like he used to. In those instances, did our past suddenly come back to him? He can certainly never have doubted my sincerity and my faithfulness. Those fleeting moments of – recaptured – grace filled me with happiness. I chased away bad memories, put them down to pressure, to the burden of his responsibilities. François was working like a madman, evenings and weekends, never letting up. At least that was what he told me.

Then, out of nowhere, he would become obnoxious again. As he did one evening in September 2013, for instance. We were having dinner outside my office, in the garden, at the foot of the giant bonsai Bernadette Chirac had bought her husband for his birthday. The following Saturday François was going to the Francophone Games in Nice. I told him I would like to go with him.

'I don't see what you would be doing there,' he replied nastily.

'It is on a Saturday evening, there will be a show, we could see it together.'

'It's not your place. The answer is no.'

I sensed it was non-negotiable, I could not understand. Not only did he not give an inch but he moved his departure forward, to make absolutely sure he would leave alone. When I guessed what his strategy was I called his Chief-of-Staff to tell her that I would be going on the trip also. François' rage intensified.

'I would rather cancel than go with you.'

I insisted. He used a visit to his father and brother as an excuse for me not to come. All the more reason.

'You erased me from your public life, now you want to erase me from your personal life – what is left for me?'

He kept stubbornly quiet.

The thought that he was meeting another woman did not cross my mind for even a second. I was overcome with despair and sought refuge in my bed. He saw how affected I was and yet he still left. I stayed alone. Suddenly remorseful, he called me to suggest that I get on a plane and join him. This time I was the one who said no.

Now that I know he was unfaithful, those memories sting. I revisit the months, the weeks. I understand what I refused to see or what he hid from me with his artful lying, an art he has been cultivating for so long. It is summer outside, I feel like scorched earth. I sleep a lot, I welcome sleep like a blessing. To sleep without dreaming, without the pain ploughing its furrow, without the anger that eats away at me … I go back to bed in the morning and sometimes even in the afternoon.

Six months have gone by already.

Every day, François begs me to see him, to start over, for us to go back to the way we were before. Every day he sends me messages saying he loves me, suggests we show ourselves in public together. I turn down all of his suggestions. Never again will there be a 'like before'. I lock myself up in my refusal to see him again. The firmer I am, the gentler his response. Too many lies, too many betrayals, too much cruelty. I have to hold out.

Manage without him. Live without him. Think without him. Love without him. I could have decided to believe him and say yes to his proposal. Come back through the main door. I could have savoured getting my own back on all those who rejoiced in my departure. It would have been intoxicating, but only fleetingly so. And then what? What sort of life would I have led on the dying embers of our burned-down love?

I would rather claw my way out of a pitch-black hole than live in the grey zone forever. I could have got the 'Madame wing' back. Instead of that I got two wings back: two wings to get off the ground.

I MEET UP with my friends from the *Secours populaire*, which never fails to kick me out of my lethargy and make me want to move forward again. We are preparing the *Secours populaire*'s 70th anniversary – it was born out of the French Resistance. I am a fan of *Secours populaire*'s philosophy and I have a lot of respect for its leaders. Julien Lauprêtre has been at the helm of *Secours pop*' for nearly sixty years. I call him 'my President'. We

met in October 2012. At the time I had just started tip-
toeing back into the Élysée Palace, following the score
of books published about me. A month later I received
a letter of apology from a man who had co-authored the
worst book of the lot. He had already wreaked havoc
with his defamations and his letter did nothing to erase
the harm he had done to me.

I had yet to find a way of making the most of my new
role as First Lady – a role which is both a beautiful and
poisoned gift. Being the President's partner, I received a
lot of gifts, mostly luxury beauty products. I wanted to
donate them to women living in poverty, but there weren't
enough of them to make the donation worthwhile. So I
called on big brand names to donate more, and they were
game. My office soon filled up with boxes. François even
asked me whether I was planning on opening up shop.

I then contacted *Secours populaire* and told them I had
a proposal to make. Julien Lauprêtre came in with three
of his collaborators. He started out by recounting his
incredible journey – the story of *Secours populaire*. I was
worried about his reaction to my idea but I went ahead
anyway. His response was full of enthusiasm: 'That is
exactly what we want – to give people their dignity back.
Why don't you come and hand the gifts out yourself?'

I explained that I was not trying to put myself forward
and that, as result of the difficult start I had got off to,

I was actively avoiding the spotlight. He convinced me to get involved regardless, and I owe him a lot for that. That day Julien Lauprêtre helped me get back on track.

And so, without any media coverage, I went to bring the beauty products to four women's shelters. I met isolated women, with their children – some had run away from domestic violence. In those lives full of misery, my perfumes and lipsticks can only have been insignificant tokens, but they were that little bit of unnecessary luxury that can help you hold your head up high.

I remember the first cheap lipstick I was able to buy – I remember how feminine it made me feel. Until then, I had borrowed lipstick from my mother or from my grandmother, Simone – from whom I also borrowed rice powder, and even though it was a down-market product I will never forget that smell. My diminutive grandmother who raised us alongside my parents – she may have been only a seamstress but she prided herself on her appearance. She truly had magic in her fingertips and I still wear some of the clothes she knitted. I have kept the crochet baby clothes she made for my children. When I think of her, I can still taste the Pulmoll sweets my brothers and sisters and I were forever knocking on her door for. Those memories made me feel close to the women I visited at the shelter. Without the money my grandmother contributed with her seamstress work, I too could have been a *Secours populaire* child. Growing up, we were lucky enough to go on holiday by the sea every year. So many children are far less fortunate.

My favourite memory of the twenty months I spent at the Élysée is my outing in Cabourg with five thousand *Secours populaire* children. I travelled by coach with the Fédération Clichy-la Garenne. We left at 7 a.m. One hundred and twenty coaches in total left for the seaside resort made famous by the French author Marcel Proust. The departure went off smoothly, with the children still half asleep. After a pit stop at a motorway rest area – apple compote and brioche snacks – the children started to get excited. They all wore a cap, colour-coded by *département* – yellow, red, blue, green. The children saw the elegant villas before they saw the sea – for the very first time.

'It's beautiful here, every family has their own house!' I heard one of them say in wonderment. Their world was their *cité*, their council housing, and most of them had never seen anything else. Another little boy said to me: 'I would really like to come back with my mum so she can see this too!'

That day, I saw the real face of poverty in France. I saw some children hide away their sandwich to bring it back and share it at home. I noticed that some of the little ones did not have bathing suits and were wearing old frayed clothes.

Before we set off, I had been wondering whether a day at the seaside was an inadequate way of helping them. I saw I had been wrong. A single day of happiness, just one day, opened their world, allowed them to see another horizon than their *cité*. In September they too would have a holiday adventure to talk about.

That day, 28 August 2013, filled me with just as much joy as it did them. François Hollande did not want to take any holidays that summer, but I got my DfH, Day for the Holidayless! The children did not know my name or what I looked like but my role had been explained to them. When the young boys and girls came to talk to me they would ask: 'Is it true that you are the President's wife? And you came to see us?'

Without the *Secours populaire*, they would just be forgotten, those who are given so few opportunities to make it, locked up in their *banlieue* council blocks, outside of town, outside of life.

I lifted my trousers up to feel the seawater. In the general melee of cameras and children, I got soaked – in fact I very nearly fell in the water! I had barely just got my balance back when a little girl pushed through the human wall to launch herself into my arms. 'I have been looking for you everywhere since this morning!' she exclaimed.

Childhood can be a time when nothing will get in the way of determination. Houssainatou did not let go of my hand all day after that, breaking the rules, because each group was meant to stay in its own spot. In the evening, saying goodbye to Houssainatou was tough. I did not know her surname but she was in all the pictures with me, clinging onto me.

When I got back to Paris I wanted to send her a picture and a little note. We had to do a little detective work. 'You looked for me up and down the beach. I looked for you in all around Île-de-France,' I wrote. She wrote back a beautiful letter. Six months later she was one of the *Secours populaire* children who came to the Élysée for Christmas.

At the end of the day, the volunteers and I stopped in Cabourg for red wine and *saucisson*.[24] That is the Socialist Party we know and love, the one I hail from.

My Élysée team and I then allowed ourselves a little break before heading back to Paris, because we were in such demand all day that we had not so much as touched any food. We tucked into a hot camembert with French fries and *andouille* in a little restaurant. Such a strange and wonderful combination really does exist!

What a beautiful day from start to end … even though the next day I was black-and-blue – a souvenir of the children's pushing and shoving and giving effusive hugs.

---

24 Dried cured sausage.

*Secours populaire* did not forget about me after François Hollande and I separated. The team leader sent me messages and the children sent me drawings. We are working on a few projects together. This summer I am going back to Ouistreham, in Normandy, with the children. I have now roped my friend Saïda into volunteering with me. She too could have been a *Secours populaire* child in Roubaix, where she was born. We share the same enthusiasm. We were lucky enough to make it.

Spending time with these little French children does not mean I cannot see beyond our borders, where, on top of poverty, tragedy and violence strike. When a child is suffering, his nationality does not matter. Every day, I fight to rescue from oblivion the young Nigerian girls kidnapped by Boko Haram. Their suffering is met with widespread indifference and yet they are the symbol of the oppression of women throughout the world. No one cares about them any more. Not the great and the good, nor the stars up in arms (for a day). Everyone lets it happen.

Just as the world stood by while thousands of women were raped in the Democratic Republic of Congo… I travelled to the DR Congo twice in two years. I discovered the tragic fate of women in that country in Dr Mukwege's hospital in Bukavu in the South Kivu region. Women are systematically assaulted there, they are raped in every village – all the time, wherever they go. Hell as painted by Jérôme Bosch, in a tropical setting. Age is not a factor. Temporary derangement does not come into it. Armed men mutilate women's reproductive organs to prevent them from giving birth. They use rape as a weapon of war.

I will never forget a seventy-year-old grandmother's account of how she no longer dared go to the fields after having been raped repeatedly. Or the 35-year-old woman telling me how she was raped by several men in front of her children and her husband, who were then killed. How could I ever forget the words and tears of that eighteen-year-old girl who was raped, with a knife stuck through her foot to prevent her from escaping? Her two-year-old girl – the child born from the rape – had also been raped. I still remember her screams when her mother started undressing her to show me her wounds.

Dr Mukwege is a deeply committed man who has seen it all but it is still as shocking to him as ever and his voice trembled when he spoke of the recent increase in the number of children being raped. His weariness was apparent, after twenty years spent sewing up women whose vaginas have been torn with broken glass bottles or with weapons.

Along with all the pictures of my humanitarian work, the faces of these women have been erased from the Élysée website, but they live on in my memory.

Dr Mukwege is under constant protection – he has twice been the target of attempted murder. In a country torn apart by civil war, denouncing a crime is in itself a crime. Women do not dare come forward and testify.

It was Osvalde Lewat, the wife of the French ambassador in Kinshasa, who introduced me to Dr Mukwege. A former journalist, Osvalde is a talented director and photographer, and we immediately got on. At the time she was supporting an association called VTA which worked as a refuge for young girls living in the street after their families accused them of witchcraft and threw them out, sometimes even subjecting them to torture. The association protects them from the inevitability of being raped while living on the street.

One day, the young girls sang for us in the embassy garden. One of them had a truly beautiful singing voice: 'No, no, we are not bewitched children.' Nearly all of the young girls were crying: music was a way of sublimating their pain. Everyone who at the embassy that day – the delegation, the embassy staff, and the journalists in attendance – felt that intense ripple of emotion: it went through us all like a wave. I went to get François: I wanted him to hear the song. The young girl sang again. The picture of that moment has been reprinted countless times. François and I are sat on a bench next to two little girls. François is staring into space: he is elsewhere.

Where?

A few months after my first visit to DR Congo, in October 2012, I returned to Kinshasa to join François Hollande for the *Sommet de la Francophonie*.[25] It was then that Osvalde introduced me to Dr Mukwege. I was immediately impressed by the doctor's charisma; he had commanding presence. It was as if his face had been modelled by his sheer humaneness.

Dr Mukwege asked me for my assistance. He did not want any money, what he wanted was for me to spread awareness about the fact that tens of thousands of women were the victims of crime and that almost nobody was doing anything about it. He was convinced that my voice would be of some use. I promised him I would get involved. We ran an opinion column in *Le Monde*, signed by a number of key figures. Through the Danielle Mitterrand Foundation, we sent four French doctors to teach and support the staff in Dr Mukwege's hospital. After that, we sent four Congolese doctors to Angers for four months.

I accompanied Dr Mukwege to the Human Rights Council for a 'fringe event', to appeal for the cause of women in the Congo. For the first time, I made a speech in front of an audience of ambassadors and NGO

25 A summit of French-speaking countries/former French colonies.

leaders. My voice trembled. I spoke again in New York, at NATO, to foreign affairs ministers. My voice was still shaky. It was the most nerve-racking experience of my life.

I asked for Dr Mukwege to be part of the French delegation so that he could meet the President in the Élysée plane, while I stayed behind in New York for twenty-four hours – at the request of the British Foreign Secretary. I was able to see François before his departure to let him know what my plans were. He did not ask me one question about what I had just accomplished. I knew that Nicolas Sarkozy had come to listen to Carla Bruni-Sarkozy. I did not ask for much, but François' repeated indifference truly was astounding.

On 6 December 2013, I continued the fight for the cause of raped women from the DR Congo. On the occasion of a summit in Paris on security issues, I organised a get-together for the wives of the African heads of state. We discussed the violence women are exposed to during armed conflicts. Osvalde, Arnaud Sélignac and I had produced a film to raise awareness and we screened it for the twenty-five spouses in attendance at our 'women's summit'. Victims came from Central Africa and Libya to testify. We all signed a charter committing to fight violence against women in the DR Congo. The Finnish Prime Minister's wife and the Japanese Prime Minister also signed the charter and I was hoping to get all the First Ladies around the world on board as well.

In the event, Nelson Mandela died that very day and naturally it made worldwide news. Unsurprisingly, the press hardly made any mention of our event. That evening, during the official dinner honouring the African heads of state, several of their wives spoke to François about our work. He was wide-eyed and seemed to be hearing about it for the first time.

Because being a First Lady does not afford any particular status – the role itself is very loosely defined and each First Lady embodies the role in her own unique way – I was still finding my footing. It was a daily learning curve: I was discovering what worked for me, and – above all – learning how to avoid negative publicity.

I have fond memories of a public holiday which my team and I spent filling boxes with books and toys for Mali. We had collected a lot of donations, dozens and dozens of kilos of donations, which the French Army sent off to Bamako and Gao. Military operations had been stepped up and it was becoming dangerous to work in the field.

My willing and able team spent that entire day cheerfully helping me sort through the gifts. Our task was to carefully divide the donations according to their recipients: schools, nurseries etc. There we were, on our hands and knees on the floor of the 'Madame corridor'. I doubt any other First Lady before me had ever been seen in that position. The Republican Guards could not believe their eyes ... and offered to help us!

Our work wasn't all rosy, though. My team and I suffered our fair share of setbacks and crushing disappointments – tragedy was always lurking around the corner. Chain of Hope was one of the organisations that came to me for help. Chain of Hope performs heart surgery on children the world over. I met with professors Alain Deloche and Éric Cheysson several times – men whom I instantly respected for their deep commitment and enthusiasm. Together, we strove to find funding to open a cardiology unit for children in Bamako. We had nearly reached our target funding when the pictures of the President with his scooter helmet on were printed. I am not sure what became of our project after that.

One of my saddest memories of the humanitarian work I carried out as First Lady was with Chain of Hope – not that the people in charge there had anything to do with it, obviously. One morning in November 2013, news broke that a Malian child named Lamina urgently needed an operation. He would die without that operation but he had neither a visa nor any funds to travel. Chain of Hope called on me for help. I in turn went to the chief military doctor at the Élysée, as he participated in our humanitarian work.

In under twenty-four hours everything had been organised for surgery to take place at the Necker children's hospital two days later. I felt like I had been handed a magic wand to save this child's life. It was a surreal and wonderful feeling.

Lamina was operated on. His father stayed on in France to wait for him, while his mother remained in Mali. Forty-eight hours later, there were complications. Lamina fell into a coma and died.

I felt responsible for his death. Though the doctors assured me that he would have died had he stayed in Mali, I cannot forgive myself for the fact that Lamina did not die in his mother's arms. I feel for that poor woman, who trusted us with her son and received a coffin by return post.

I felt so powerless I was tempted to give it all up. My team rallied to cheer me up and the doctors did their best to find the words to console me – they were experienced in dealing with this sort of situation. I was not. I was utterly unprepared for such grief.

Being a First Lady also sometimes means being someone's last resort. One evening while I was alone at our home on rue Cauchy, a young woman got in touch on Twitter. I answered. Sensing her anguish, I asked her for her phone number. When I called her, she responded in a barely audible voice, repeating only these words:

'I want to die!' I could not get her to engage with me and eventually suggested that she write to me what she could not put into words. I gave her my email address but all I received were fragments of sentences – the tone was always the same. I had her details so I passed them on to my Chief-of-Staff Patrice Biancone, asking him to get an Élysée doctor or the social services involved. In our email exchanges, the woman, who was a respected lecturer, had given me the address of the place she was staying: it was a cheap suburban hotel.

The next day she sent me an alarming email: 'Thank you for everything, Valérie, I want to say goodbye.' Patrice and I got the hotel to break her door down. She was unconscious when they found her. The fire brigade managed to save her just in time – despite the lethal mix she had swallowed: detergents, medicine and alcohol. She spent three months in hospital. Fate sometimes plays strange tricks on us: three months later it was my turn to spend some time in hospital and, that time, she was the one who got in touch to support me. We write regularly now. I have often wondered since whether I did the right thing when I responded to her SOS. Was she really suicidal or was it a cry for help – because she knew she had a sympathetic ear in me? How can you ever know?

Being a First Lady means dealing with all sorts of situations.

My staff was certainly smaller than any other First Lady team before it and therefore far less expensive – which did not stop critics from finding fault with it on the basis that it was funded with public money. Yet it would be unfair to accuse my team of sitting around twiddling our thumbs: over the two years we worked together, we received countless – non-stop – requests of every possible nature. The President's staff even called on me for matters that would normally be dealt with by human resources. They knew I was on their side.

While humanitarian organisations always saw the useful side of my role, public opinion was not on my side. From day one, in the eyes of many French citizens, I was illegitimate. I had taken a spot saved for another woman, with a prophetic name that spelled out her destiny – a Madonna figure to boot.

Under the crossfire of information channels and social networks, my journey at the Élysée was paved with accusations. I would regularly discover that I had been summoned to appear before a judge for misappropriation of public funds. With time, as the expression goes, the skin thickens and the heart hardens. But those who claim indifference are lying – being deeply unpopular hurts.

A few seconds of a broadcast about a two-day trip the President made to Dijon in March 2013, for instance, were a cruel stab in the back for me. The trip was his team's idea

– a bid to help him restore a healthy relationship with the French people at a time when his popularity ratings were free-falling. The operation was a fiasco for him, and it was brutally painful for me. While the cameras were filming the President, an elderly lady came up to him in the street and said: 'Don't marry Valérie, we don't like her.'

It was hardly tactful on her part, but after all she is free to say what she wants. Her pique was nothing next to François' roar of laughter … My God, how I resented him in that moment! His cowardice prevented him from uttering a single sentence in my defence – or even just a kind word to dodge her comment – something he is usually so skilled at doing. It had me in tears in front of my television set.

Ever mindful of his own popularity – which was melting like butter in the sun – he could not care less what was said of me. Meanwhile, I had never let a scornful attack against him or an insult go unanswered. One winter Sunday, for example, as we were walking down the embankment near our flat, a passer-by heckled François twice in a row. François had to grab me by the arm to keep me from turning around and demanding an explanation. We went home in deadly silence. From that day on, there would be no more walks for us: François could not stand confrontation. And he knew all too well that the *banlieue* girl in me could resurface at any moment, as she had one day right before an election, when I shouted: 'Come and say it here, arsehole,' to a man who had just verbally assaulted François.

Six months later, the Léonarda case was one of the four or five moments in François Hollande's mandate that lastingly dented his image – and I played a part in it, albeit a minor one. At the start of the school year, in September 2013, I had decided to read the ELA dictation in my old school, in Angers. The headmistress signed off on it and two of my old schoolteachers made the journey especially. One of them had meant a lot to me as a child. She was beautiful and she fascinated me. I wanted her to like me, and I wanted to be like her. That was almost forty years ago…

In those years, the school was in an area that had been earmarked as an urbanisation priority; things have not much changed since then. The Paul Valéry School had a lot of children of refugees, many of whom did not speak French fluently. The ELA team came with me, as well as a small boy who was severely disabled.

That day the 'Léonarda case' was all over the news: a teenage girl illegally living in France was deported to Kosovo with her family. Some high school students were protesting against the deportation order. I guessed that I would be asked to comment, and had prepared a balanced answer which I felt would avoid stirring up the controversy: 'School is a place of integration, not exclusion, as it should be for disabled children.'

The second part of my answer was of no interest to the press and was widely ignored. I also said that Léonarda was not responsible for her father's actions. No child should be held accountable for their parents' wrongdoings. I was shocked that the police made that child come out of her school bus in front of her classmates.

I was immediately accused of stoking the fire. François' rage stunned me like a slap in the face. He refused to see me when I got back, but I insisted that he found a moment so we could talk. He finally agreed to talk … to berate me for having made a statement before him. I was astounded. 'So you plan on making a statement about the case?' I asked.

'Nothing has been decided yet, but yes, I will probably say something tomorrow.'

It did not seem like a good idea to me but I did not dare say as much. At that point, the President had not yet reached a decision: should the family be deported or not? He was undecided. He had a war on his hands between his Prime Minister and his Minister of the Interior and he had to find a way to make peace. I shyly suggested a solution: 'What about the little girl? Can't she finish school in France in a boarding school – as sometimes happens for isolated minors?'

'No, that's impossible,' he answered with a shrug of his shoulders.

The next morning he had still not decided what to do. When I set off for La Lanterne to cycle, I saw the PM's and the Minister of the Interior's cars arrive through the garden gate. I cycled for longer that day. It was nearly one in the afternoon when I got back. I listened to the radio while I was in the shower and it was only then that I heard François was going to make a statement. He had not told me. I quickly switched on the television. I had absolutely no idea what he was going to say. I found out that he had gone with my suggestion, which he had ruled out as idiotic just the day before. In fact, it was not a choice he was making but a way of circumventing a clash between the Prime Minister and the Minister of the Interior.

François' statement caused an outcry. Politicians and editorial writers alike fell tooth and nail on the President. His proposal that Léonarda should be allowed to stay was not understood, it was seen as an act of weakness. Protecting children seems like a brave decision to me and even though it was unpopular, I am grateful to him for his proposal.

A month later I was awarding the Prize for the Danielle Mitterrand Foundation and I prepared a speech listing the actions I had carried out in her name. At the end of that list, I paid her homage by trying to imagine what the wife of the first Socialist President would have said in 2013 if she was still will us: 'Would Danielle Mitterrand have kept quiet about the tragedy of the women who are victims of rape in the Democratic Republic of Congo? Would Danielle Mitterrand have kept quiet about Syria's tragedy and its refugees?' I ended my speech with the sentence: 'I will be quiet no longer' – a reference to the Breaking the Silence campaign to support raped women.

The AFP flouted the whole speech, keeping only that very last bit – taking it completely out of context. In a show of immense bad faith, the AFP interpreted my sentence as a statement about the Léonarda case, a reminder of the tweet during the La Rochelle election, and a desire to take part in the political debate again. Christmas come early again for the web and the news channels.

The mood at the Élysée that evening was stormy. Once again, I faced a volley of criticism – an uninterrupted flow of hurtful comments … all the way to our bed. I could not take it any more. François never paid me a compliment, never uttered a word of support – only cruel words of reproach came out of his mouth. It was almost midnight but I decided to get dressed and leave.

François first tried to stop me, then said he would call a driver. I left alone, walking out through the *Court d'honneur*. I did not look down to hide my tear-filled eyes in front of the policemen who gave me a polite nod when I walked through the gate. I left with no money, just the keys to rue Cauchy in my pocket.

Two minutes later, my phone started ringing non-stop. François and my security guard were both concerned for my safety. I did not pick up. I walked all the way to rue Cauchy. It took me almost an hour. It did me good to be back in the shelter of my own home.

The next morning, the AFP issued an amended version of its article, François admitted that he had been wrong and recognised that my speech had been unfairly reported on.

Now that we have separated, I can barely believe all those arguments. Some of them tore us apart. In May 2013, I decided to leave François. He was too hard, I could not take his cruelty anymore. I went back to the flat on rue Cauchy and forbade him from coming back to it. We did not see each other for three weeks. Every weekend I would go away with friends – I essentially toured France. But in the end I came back to him. I was addicted to him.

Not for a minute did I imagine that he had made the most of his freedom to see another woman. Faithful women are forever naive…

The man wooing me today – as he did when we first met – is nothing like the cutting partner I remember. He has become attentive again, as if he had managed to melt that 'frozen sea' inside him – Kafka's metaphor for our inner fortress. The man who had become so stingy with his compliments has only words of praise about me these days. He notices everything I do, always knows where I am, encourages me with any initiative I take and has congratulated me on the short interviews I gave for *Secours populaire*, as well as those I gave about the Nigerian schoolgirls.

When we lived together, he did not even know the name of the show I presented on television! The most surprising of all is that he even makes the effort to read my book reviews in *Paris-Match* … on top of the political pages!

The overworked, overbooked and indifferent President has morphed into an attentive President who finds the time to read everything that is printed about me and send me dozen of texts – including when he is in a meeting at the Élysée. The mind boggles! Now that I am resisting his attempts to win me over, I have renewed market value in the eyes of a man whose motivation is to conquer.

IN DECEMBER 2013, after Nelson Mandela was taken to hospital in a critical state, I told François that I wanted to accompany him to the funeral. In response he served up his now-famous: 'I don't see why you would be there.'

I replied that I would go no matter what, I would use my press card and pay for my flight. On the morning

'Madiba' died I was too afraid he would send me packing and did not dare bring up the subject over breakfast. I sent him a text during the day. He agreed that I could come. I later learned that it had not been his decision. The diplomats insisted that I be part of the trip as Barack Obama and most of the heads of state were going to the funeral with their spouses.

I was moved at the thought of attending the ceremony. We had just returned from Brazil and Guyana when we had to leave again, followed by a second plane that Nicolas Sarkozy chartered for himself. At the airport, François said he was thinking of inviting his predecessor in his car, while I would ride in another car. I served him straight up: 'Do you think he would have stood Carla up for you?' My answer left him speechless and I rode in his car with him. François ignored me in the stadium. In his eyes, Nicolas Sarkozy was the only person who mattered. I kept my distance to let them speak freely. The former President was the one who came to find me and introduced me to the other heads of state.

François and Nicolas Sarkozy were both laughing. Their behaviour struck me as rather inappropriate, and I scowled at them. In pictures released in the press, I look like a mother keeping an eye on her misbehaving children… Like two veterans reuniting, they talked about the hardships of the job: the bad ministers, the lack of holidays, the attacks. Nicolas Sarkozy described the sumptuous property that the King of Morocco made available to him and his family. None of the pressing current affairs was more important than that to the two of them.

Was this public bonding befitting, given the circumstances? We were at Nelson Mandela's funeral, which was being broadcast across the world. And the two frenemies were having a ball. Nicolas Sarkozy was leading the dance. It made me uncomfortable to see François behaving that way with him. I said as much. In a raised voice, he swore he would never take me on an official visit ever again.

Thankfully, the arrival of the US presidents – former and incumbent – helped ease the tension between the two of us. In a matter of minutes, I saw Barack and Michelle Obama, Bill and Hillary Clinton and the Bushes arrive – I was star-struck. I shook Barack Obama's hand for the first time. He looked me straight in the eyes with his very own brand of unapologetic directness. But again, it was Michelle Obama who really captured my attention. She fascinated me: she was mesmerisingly charismatic.

During the ceremony, a picture of the US President's selfie with the blonde Danish Prime Minister started going around the world. Next to me, I noticed Michelle's brooding expression, and I liked her even more! I was delighted to see I was not the only jealous partner.

I will readily admit to it: I am jealous. I have been

jealous with every man I have loved. I do not know how not to be when I am in love.

I was jealous with François as I had never been before – because I loved him more than I had ever loved any man before him. I could not stand seeing other women put their heads on his shoulder and hold him by the waist to take a photo with him. I certainly did not like that. I have even sent a few of them packing. Would these women have liked me to cosy up to their husbands?

Cécilia Attias, Nicolas Sarkozy's ex-wife, has said that she would often see women give her husband their phone number. Her conclusion was that nothing will stop a woman attracted by power. What a sad statement, yet so true.

I was unfairly tried as a woman drawn like a moth to the spotlight of power. Those prosecuting me must have forgotten that I fell in love with a man who – when the pollsters even remembered to include him on the list of potential candidates – only scored 3 per cent of potential votes in the polls. Had I been placing a bet, there were certainly horses with better odds! My relationship with François could hardly be compared with the way some women swoon over a President between two international summits.

Oddly, none of those who criticised my possessiveness ever mentioned François' jealousy, which was just as debilitating. He has more self-control and was therefore better at hiding it in public. But in private, he was unforgiving. To this day, even after having brutally offloaded me from his life, he cannot stand the thought that I could be with another man.

The gossip columnists write that he feels liberated and is happy as Larry. Strange, then, that as soon as the media alleges I have a new lover, his messages take on an extremely aggressive tone… Once, after seeing a picture of me next to another man, he had the audacity to send me the following message: 'It's over between us.'

'Thanks,' I wrote back, 'I've been aware of it since 25 January – as has the rest of the world.' Double standards, as always. How many women does he need in his harem?

On public outings François never had cause to worry, which meant he never had to keep his jealousy in check. No one ever took any liberties with me. I was often chastised for keeping my distance. Personally, I would have preferred François to do the same, and told him as much time and time again – as did all his advisers. 'Being friendly' does not a President make. But he could not help himself, it was second-nature to him – since childhood he had been the life and soul of a group, its jester leader.

François was just as hopeless in his dealings with the media, which he flooded with messages. Political journalists started to keep track of how many of them were receiving text messages from the President. The figure is astounding: over seventy! Any journalist investigating a minister or a minor case is entitled to an audience with the President. Ever since he took his first steps in politics, he cajoles them, even those who have dragged him through the mud. He never gives up.

He is a politician who likes to play journalist. Speaking as a political journalist, such absolute fusion with the media is unheard of. Even Nicolas Sarkozy was more distant with the media, which is saying something!

This frenzy absorbs much of his energy and plays against him. François simply cannot resist the appeal of a microphone placed in front of him, of a camera zooming in on him, waiting, expectantly, for a sound bite or a bon mot. Many a time I have watched him ruin a successful political Q&A by subsequently answering off-topic questions, badly framed by the camera, in a dark and dimly lit corner surrounded by a multitude of microphones. He might have given an excellent speech prior to that but all that would run in the media would be two or three badly strung sentences.

I remember a scene in Moscow that would have had anyone tearing their hair out in despair. His team explained that he should not make any public statements before meeting Putin. 'Obviously,' he said. Only to run to the cameras ten minutes later!

I soon threw in the towel.

And yet it is abroad that I think he is at his best. Other than a couple of slips of the tongue caused by jet lag, he was never caught out on figures or the history of a country. He was impressive. And I do have reference points, having covered as a journalist some of former Prime Minister Lionel Jospin's and former President Jacques Chirac's official visits.

On state visits, without fail, I was completely enthralled to see him reviewing the troops to the beat of various national anthems. His tie might have been a little wonky – I could not have cared less. All I saw was how far he had come. I could not take my eyes off him. I was like a spectator watching him in a film.

There is something almost romantic about state visits: it is like being the hero of a novel, they are the rewards of a back-breaking role. The most wonderful of all was the state visit to Japan. I have enchanted memories of our welcome by the Emperor and the Empress. How could a little girl from a *banlieue* outside of Angers ever have imagined that one day the Empress of Japan would ask her if they could address each other by their first names? I could not bring myself to address her by any other title than 'Your Majesty'. She was aware of the social work I did and gave me a kiss on the cheek in front of the cameras when we were leaving. I was expecting critics to berate me for not observing protocol. But, that time, they held back.

When the French ministers went to pay their respects to the imperial couple, François and I shared a moment. The Chief of Protocol had briefed them on how to bow down slightly before walking away, never turning their back. Some of them were so flustered and clumsy that François and I started giggling uncontrollably.

In late 2013, and despite our altercations and our fights, a strong bond still united us. Between two quarrels, we shared real moments of tenderness and were still attracted to one another. One minute we tore each other apart and the next we would make up, passionately. This is why I thought we were unbreakable.

Before I saw the pictures of François on his way to meet his mistress, I would have staked my life on the fact that he would never betray me or abandon me – that he would never do such a thing to me, not in a million years.

But he did and I still cannot get over it. I will not get over it.

## 4 July 2014

Twenty-nine. I counted them: he sent me twenty-nine text messages yesterday. All through his Friday as President of France, despite his timed-to-the minute schedule,

François Hollande sent me twenty-nine text messages. I blame myself for having replied to him and stoked the fire. We are going around in circles, as we do every day. What he says to me is always the same: he wants me back and we should start over. My answer is invariably the same: he crushed me, he put me down, and did nothing to help me get back up.

François still swears that he has not seen Julie Gayet since January or had any contact with her. What does he tell *her*? What does he write to her? What did he tell her about me during their clandestine affair? That he did not love me any more? That I was impossible? That our relationship was platonic? Cowardice is the great unifier of unfaithful men, and men in power.

These last few years have made me far more committed. Where previously I only had opinions, I now act on them. I am involved. Though I no longer represent France, or anything else for that matter, I am almost as sought after by the media and various organisations as I was during my time at the Élysée. It rather amuses me to read, now, about Valérie Trierweiler 'the ex-First Lady'; whereas when I had an office at the Élysée I was only 'François Hollande's partner'. I became a First Lady in the eyes of the media the day I effectively stopped being one. The role stays with the women who have embodied it. She may have divorced him six months into Nicolas Sarkozy's five-year presidential term, but Cécilia Attias remains a former First Lady, just as surely as Anne-Aymone Giscard d'Estaing, Bernadette Chirac and Carla Bruni-Sarkozy.

Should I have behaved differently? Some would have wanted me to be no more than a silent puppet, walking in the President's footsteps, mute, submissive and essentially invisible. But I was not prepared to do that and while I was able to preserve part of who I was and say what I thought, I certainly paid a heavy price for it. The past two years have been marred by misunderstandings and the negative public image that clung to me like a bad smell.

Since our separation, I have noticed that people no longer look at me in the same way. Women everywhere express support, in the name of sisterhood.

My actions are heartfelt – I have not given up hope that one day my sincerity will no longer be under scrutiny. The seeds that I sowed at the Élysée have grown.

Today, I received two bouquets. One brought to me in the street by a little girl called Elisa – her family had sent her; they wanted to let me know they were supportive of what I had been through. The second one was left in front of my door by one of my Twitter followers. I have never met her, she is a retired school teacher who defends me tooth and nail online. I am so touched. Every passing day brings with it a new solace.

I could have shied away from the First Lady position – the thought did cross my mind. I could have refused to step inside the Élysée, I could have refused to accompany the President on his official visits. It would not have made much of a difference to the controversies, the insinuations and the basic serialisation of our story in the media. Besides, there would have been a missing piece in the puzzle. Protocol demands that France be represented as a twosome. And the symbolic function of First Lady is important in our country, even if it does bring with it scandalmongering and a whole host of unfounded assumptions and accusations – and the trial is never fair.

I have not kept any of the magnificent presents I received. The Rolex watches and other Chopard jewellery have been safely stored in the official safes, at the Quai Branly Museum. I had three different witnesses sign the proof that I had returned these presents to the French Republic. You can never be too careful when, like me, you have learned that in politics everything – and I mean everything – goes.

I do not represent anything any more; I am not a candidate for anything. Now that I no longer have an official title, I can freely back causes and struggles that I believe are just. I am a free woman and I want to continue to make myself useful. 'Useful' is such a beautiful word – humbling and empowering at the same time.

Ukrainians living in France and Syrian refugees come to see me. 'Help us,' they say, 'come to our country, see it for yourself.' Of course, I have no scope for action in international crises. But I can use my voice to echo and magnify other voices. I am a journalist and I want to get out of my office, I want to see with my own eyes, and then describe what I have seen. I have visited refugee camps in Lebanon, slums in India, in South Africa and in Haiti – as well as in France, where some travellers' settlements are worse still. I can write and say what I want.

Until now, I have avoided broadcasting any of my political opinions about François' policies. The way public affairs have drifted saddens me enormously. From what I see and what I hear, politics holds nothing that can attract me at the moment. I cannot keep track of the number of times he has flip-flopped … I know how he hesitates and plays for time – only to quietly do a U-turn without feeling like he owes anyone an explanation. Does he still know which side is left?

It is always the weak I think of first when an economic decision is made or when large-scale redundancies are announced – François once berated me for saying I was a 'left-wing woman' on TV. At the time, I had not understood what he was accusing me of. I was born on the side of the weakest social strata. Those who have to count every euro. That is where I come from. And those are the people I think of first when an economic decision is made or when large-scale redundancies are announced. I know that life is going to be that much harder on them.

Would François Hollande have preferred me to say: 'I am a right-wing woman'? Obviously not. I think what he wanted – above all else – was for me to keep my mouth shut. He wanted me to be nothing more than his lover – an immaculate, untarnished, mute figure. I had the misfortune of not being the rounded, polished and sweet woman he would have liked to have beside him when he finally obtained supreme power.

I remember a conversation he and I had before the Socialist primaries. François had spent a few days in hospital for a minor operation. For a hyperactive man like him, it takes being stuck on a hospital bed to remember what is important.

That day, he let his guard down and we had the most profound conversation we had ever had. He admitted having suffered from having been one half of a political power couple. He confided that it wasn't his choice, that it had been circumstantial and compounded by Ségolène Royal's ambition, which became more and more entrenched as the years went by.

That day, François, who is usually so secretive and never opens up about his past, told me how much he had suffered from having to share the political spotlight with – and sometimes be in the shadow of – the mother of his children. It all started when François Mitterrand appointed Ségolène Royal – leaving him out of the Cabinet. His name had been struck off the list at the last minute because the President did not want a couple in his government.

I also remember a story, back in the day when I was a young political journalist and François Hollande a freshly elected MP. He and I were talking, at a garden party held at the Élysée for Bastille Day, at the time François Mitterrand was the President of France. Not far off, Ségolène Royal was being showered with attention. A guest walked towards François, handshake extended: 'Hello, Mr Royal!' he said.

François smiled back, coldly. After the rude man had left, François said under his breath: 'That's not the end of that.'

Fifteen years later, I was by his side when Ségolène Royal rose to become the Socialist Party's presidential candidate of choice – when he was the party's First Secretary – and I know how trying that was for his ego.

That day, in his hospital room, I thought he was talking about his past. But he may have been addressing me, too.

I was not sure where he was going with it all. Our enchanted years were coming to an end. He was about to announce he was running for President and the odds were in his favour. He did not want to share any of it with anyone else. Declaring myself a Socialist woman on television, existing outside of his control, was like plunging him back into his life with Ségolène Royal and the frustration he endured. I remember him flying into a rage about a magazine cover where we featured together. 'You take up all the space!'

The reaction of a wounded man.

I paid the price for his past, that political twosome that time after time ruined our daily lives, as well as proving to be an obstacle to our future together.

At the same time – and this is the 'Hollande contradiction' – a man who refused to share the spotlight, who wanted to star in a one-man show, that very same man, was the one who fell in love with a woman who had a job, a life, three children and an independent and free spirit. He could have found someone more accommodating. Instead, he chose an all-consuming love. That is the way of politicians, those strong and egocentric individuals who want it all – one thing and then the other – because their ambitions are limitless.

In any case, he does not have me completely fooled: I know full well that in some circumstances showcasing me served his purpose. When the time came to vote on the law opening up marriage to same-sex couples – the so-called 'marriage for all' law – François did not lose sight of the promises he had made; and this in spite of huge street protests. Deep down, he himself was not fully convinced – citing the 'mayors' freedom of conscience'. The second I heard that he was playing with the idea of a 'conscientious objection' proviso, I sent him a message warning him that his sentence would not go down well. Faced with an outcry, as I had predicted, he took it out of his rhetoric.

In this particular battle, I was on the front line, with his approval and maybe even in his stead. Probably because he sees marriage as an anachronism, François has never fully grasped – he understands it only on an intellectual level – just how far-reaching this emblematic Socialist reform of France's marriage laws is. In fact, it will likely be his only lasting mark in France's history books. The irony of this is not lost on me.

François sends me text messages saying that I am the woman of his life. I have heard that expression before. He used it about me in an interview, shortly before back-tracking. Once duplicitous, always duplicitous…

A few weeks ago, he asked me to marry him. It is the third time. The first time was in 2010, but my divorce was too recent, I wasn't ready. The second time was after he was elected, in September 2012. We had even discussed getting married before Christmas in a very small ceremony, in Tulle. He pulled out a month before the date and spoke words of inhuman cruelty. Julie Gayet was already a part of his life, but I did not know that then.

It is too late. You do not get married to make amends. Naturally, being married to him would have made my life much easier. In other people's minds, and possibly in mine too, I would have had more legitimacy. This official bond would no doubt have set my mind at rest and I would not have lost my self-confidence. I did not need two rings, but I needed him and I to be in the same circle of trust.

I recently went to the theatre with my youngest son to see Victor Hugo's play *Lucrèce Borgia* at the Comédie-Française. That night, with a choked heart, I drowned in Lucrèce's speech to her husband, Don Alphonso: 'You have let the people ridicule me, you have let them insult me … Who weds, protects.' Tragedy is eternal.

At François Hollande's side, I went through many lows as well as thrilling highs, I met unforgettable people and lived very intense moments. That person – who is supposedly me, a product of circumstances and media frenzy – no longer has any reason to exist. This book is a message in a bottle – in it lies my past with him. I have made mistakes, I sometimes lost my way, I might even have behaved in a hurtful way, but I never put on an act, I was never anyone but myself, I was always sincere.

Everything I have written in this book is true. I suffered

too much from lies to be untruthful myself. Writing helped me deal with the fruits of my anger and disappointment. How much longer will I be mourning this love? The President summarised our relationship in eighteen ice-cold words, which he himself dictated to the AFP. These pages are my own answer. The full stop to our relationship. They will be read only by those who want to understand me. The others will walk on by, without stopping, and that is as it should be.

The time has come to end this story, written through my tears, my sleepless nights and my memories – some wounds have healed, some still hurt. Thank you for this moment, thank you for this mad love, thank you for this trip to the Élysée. But not only that. Thank you, also, for the chasm of despair you pushed me into. You taught me a lot about you, about others and about myself. I can now be and do as I please without fearing people's judgement of me, without pleading for you to only *see* me. I want to live, I want to write more pages in this strange book that is life, I want to continue on this singular voyage that is a woman's life. You will not be a part of it. You neither married nor protected me.

Would that I was loved as much as I have loved.

# AUTHOR'S

# ACKNOWLEDGEMENTS

I WOULD LIKE TO express my heartfelt thanks to my editor, Laurent Beccaria, who followed the writing of this memoir from beginning to end, giving me considerable latitude – which was what I needed. Without ever putting any pressure on me, he found a way to take on board my frailty and guided me when I needed – always with generosity.

Thank you, Anna Jarota, my literary agent, who, on top of her professionalism, supported me as a friend would.

I am also grateful to four people who are close to me for keeping the secret about the book I was writing. I would like to apologise to my friends and family whom I did not let into the secret.

Lastly, thank you to all the people who have written to me and whom I have not had time to reply to – I want them to know that I read their letters, that they moved me and helped me hold on and get back on my feet.

*Paris,*
*31 July 2014*

**READY** *for* **HILLARY?**

PORTRAIT OF A
PRESIDENT IN
WAITING

ROBIN RENWICK

256PP HARDBACK, £17.99

Clinton was the first First Lady to have her ... West Wing of the White House and the only ... to be subpoenaed to testify before a grand jury. Upon leaving the White House, she was elected as the first female Senator for New York, then served as one of America's most popular Secretaries of State.

Hillary is poised to decide whether she will launch a fresh attempt to take the highest office in the world and make history in doing so. But what is Hillary really like? Will she run? Can she win? What can the world expect from Hillary if she does get back to the White House? What sort of President would she be?

Robin Renwick, who was the British ambassador in Washington when the Clintons arrived in the White House, seeks to answer these questions and more in this vivid portrait of one of the most polarising and central figures in recent US political history.

— AVAILABLE FROM ALL GOOD BOOKSHOPS —

ALSO AVAILABLE FROM BITEBACK PUBLISHING

320PP HARDBACK, £20

## Lady Constance Lytton (1869–1923) was the most unlikely of suffragettes.

One of the elite, she was the daughter of a Viceroy of India and a lady in waiting to the Queen. She grew up in the family home of Knebworth and in embassies around the world. For forty years, she did nothing but devote herself to her family, denying herself the love of her life and possible careers as a musician or a reviewer. Then came a chance encounter with a suffragette. Constance was intrigued; witnessing Emmeline and Christabel Pankhurst on trial convinced her of the urgent necessity of votes for women and she went to prison for the cause as gleefully as any child going on a school trip.

In this extraordinary new biography, Lyndsey Jenkins reveals for the first time the fascinating story of the woman who abandoned a life of privilege to fight for women's rights.

— AVAILABLE FROM ALL GOOD BOOKSHOPS —

WWW.BITEBACKPUBLISHING.COM

ALSO AVAILABLE FROM BITEBACK PUBLISHING

DOWN WITH THE ROYALS
JOAN SMITH

WHAT HAVE THE IMMIGRANTS
EVER DONE FOR US?
KELVIN MACKENZIE

WHY WOMEN NEED QUOTAS
VICKY PRYCE

HARDBACK, £10

# PROVOCATIONS

A groundbreaking new series of short polemics composed
by some of the most intriguing voices in contemporary
culture and edited by Yasmin Alibhai-Brown.

### DOWN WITH THE ROYALS

Joan Smith argues that it has become nearly impossible to question the existence of
the monarchy. Articulate republicans are drowned out while the supercharged PR and
media machines ask only who designed Kate's dresses.

### WHAT HAVE THE IMMIGRANTS EVER DONE FOR US?

The time has come to ask what the immigrants have ever done for us — although
perhaps it would be more apt to ask what we would do without them.

### WHY WOMEN NEED QUOTAS

By failing to remove the barriers to female progression, we're starving the UK of the
talent it needs to grow and prosper to its full potential. Ultimately, Vicky Pryce argues,
there is only one solution: women need quotas.

— AVAILABLE FROM ALL GOOD BOOKSHOPS —

WWW.BITEBACKPUBLISHING.COM

ALSO AVAILABLE FROM BITEBACK PUBLISHING

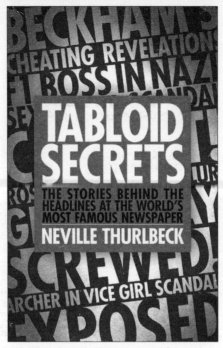

336PP HARDBACK, £16.99

**Both as chief reporter and news editor for nearly twenty years at the now defunct *News of the World*, Neville Thurlbeck is uniquely placed to give an insider's view of life on the paper.**

Thurlbeck served up some of the most famous, memorable and notorious headlines in the paper's existence; headlines that lit up the world of tabloid journalism and featured names such as David Beckham, Jeffrey Archer, Fred and Rose West, Gordon Brown and Robin Cook, among many others. In *Tabloid Secrets*, he reveals for the very first time how he broke the award-winning stories that thrilled, excited and shocked the nation, and secured the paper up to fifteen million readers every week.

Ultimately, *Tabloid Secrets* is a journey through a world that has vanished for good, by the best-known reporter of recent times. It is a vivid, surprising and wildly entertaining insider account of a Fleet Street that is suddenly no more.

— AVAILABLE FROM ALL GOOD BOOKSHOPS —

WWW.BITEBACKPUBLISHING.COM

**POLITICOS**.co.uk
THE ONLINE POLITICAL BOOKSTORE

**AN ONLINE COMMUNITY OF
POLITICAL BOOK LOVERS**

BREAKDOWNS OF THE
BEST POLITICAL
LITERATURE ON
THE HORIZON

**SPECIALIST, CONSTANTLY UPDATED
POLITICAL CONTENT**

TAILORED BESTSELLER
LISTS FROM RECESS
READING TO POLITICAL
RESEARCH MATERIALS

THE POLITICOS.CO.UK
TEAM ON HAND TO
OFFER YOU GUIDANCE
AND BESPOKE
BOOK SUGGESTIONS

WEEKLY POLITICAL
BOOK PODCASTS

Join the debate on Twitter and Facebook.

@Politicos_co_uk  www.facebook.com/politicoscouk